ASCENT
OF THE
INNER EVEREST

LEONARD MOULES

CHRISTIAN LITERATURE CRUSADE

CHRISTIAN LITERATURE CRUSADE
The Dean, Alresford, Hants.

U.S.A.
Box C, Fort Washington, Pennsylvania 19034.

AUSTRALIA
Box 91, Pennant Hills, N.S.W. 2120.

NEW ZEALAND
Box 1688, Auckland, C.1.

also in

Europe, Canada,
Central America, South America,
West Indies, Africa, India,
Indonesia, Far East

© 1971
Christian Literature Crusade

Published 1971

SBN 900284 28 5

Printed in England by Plowprint, London, S.E.18

When I think of the huge sums of money spent on that mountain, the vast supplies marshalled for the thirteen attempts upon Everest, and the human energies poured out — and then reflect . . .

I cannot but wish that men might spend with equal ardour on the "Inner Everest" what is so lavishly devoted to the outer.

W. H. Murray
Deputy Leader of Everest Expedition
1951

From the foreword of *Some Want it Tough*
by Len Moules

BY THE SAME AUTHOR

Some Want it Tough

Then God Stepped In

This is no Accident

My Quiet Time

Guidance and Temptation

Can I Trust My Bible

Three Miles High (out of print)

Acknowledgment is made to Messrs Hodder and Stoughton Limited for permission to quote from *Ascent of Everest* by Sir John Hunt and *High Adventure* by Sir Edmund Hillary: also to Rev. John L. Bird for the use of his article.

Scripture references are taken from the *Authorised Version*, the *Revised Standard Version* and from modern translations, where the interpretation has not been prejudiced, as follows: the *Amplified Bible* published by Marshall, Morgan and Scott Limited, *The New Testament* by J. B. Phillips published by Wm. Collins Sons & Co. Ltd., and *N.E.B.*, second edition © 1970 by permission of Oxford and Cambridge University Presses.

Key to the book

It is natural for me to equate the Christian life with a mountaineering expedition. I love mountains. The major portion of twenty years' missionary service has been in the High Himalaya. The tangled mass of eternal snows, glaciers, ice falls and deep valleys was the world of my missionary commission. I lived amongst remote people who were simple, honest, brave and hardworking. They came to accept me. Some came to accept my Saviour.

Three expeditions visited our Himalaya. I watched with intense interest the bearded mountaineers preceding several mules of the expedition's transport. Nanda Devi, Nanda Kot or Panchchhuli were about to see man's siege and assault. These are unforgettable memories of late night talks around the expeditions' camp fires. I listened to plans of assault or contributed advice on weather and local custom. I longed to climb with them. They would have welcomed me in a support role. But the Lord Jesus Christ's call was dominant over all other calls. I climbed high for God and for souls. This spiritual purpose embracing the challenge and danger of living high made life so utterly satisfying and worth while.

Life to me is one great expedition. It is the ascent of a personal inner Everest. My experiences of God are also pages of a living theological thesis. Often I have been confused by the loose usage of spiritual terminology; sometimes baffled by the fixed terms of reference to special "blessings". Thus I look back through forty years of walking with Jesus as the predominant Personality in my life. He has led me in an ordered way — in spite of myself!

To David, the Psalmist, the Lord was his Shepherd. To Paul, the call of Christ was involvement as a soldier, or as an athlete in the games. Have not I a similar privilege to see in Jesus Christ my Guide and Climbing Companion? This is the viewpoint of this book.

These studies have been shared at Youth camps, also at a convention for the deepening of the spiritual life at Bethany Fellowship, Minneapolis, U.S.A. I am now asked to help others to climb. It may tend to lose that anointed personal touch by appearing in cold print, but I have just risen from my knees after prayer to our mighty God through Jesus Christ for that enabling to help you climb high on your own Inner Everest.

Len Moules

April 15th, 1970.

PART ONE

THE PREPARATION

Contents

1

The Perspective

THE SUMMIT looked so near but I was not deceived. It would take at least another ten short climbs of ten lung-bursting paces apiece. Then five minutes' rest between each attempt to ease the hammering heart. An hour later I stood gazing out over a new world — a beautiful world of pure ice and snow. It was a summit experience.

Is there a similar spiritual summit, an Inner Everest — an Absolute? We had been searching the Scriptures and examining Christian experience at our morning devotional sessions in W.E.C. Headquarters. Our findings were that a summit is acknowledged by all who experience Christian discipleship. Not that they attain it, or climb high, but that it is there. The Scriptures point to a peak. The Lord Jesus Christ came to reveal His Ultimate. The Holy Spirit came as the Ability to reach it. So to the Christian there is an Absolute. Not as in the philosophies and reasonings of men who point to a "higher" and fail to see the "highest"; this is the extremity of the best of humanism and human moralities. Christ set a Summit for His mountaineers. "The One who called you is holy; like him, be holy in all your behaviour, because Scripture says 'You shall be holy, for I am holy'" (1 Pet. 1:15).

The inner cry of the Christian confirms this Absolute. St. Paul sincerely cried, "All I care for is to know Christ, to experience the power of his resurrection, and to share his sufferings, in growing conformity with his death, if only I may finally arrive at the resurrection from the dead" (Phil. 3: 10). On the plane-table of human life the Great Surveyor marks the trig-point of the highest altitude with these words, "This is eternal life: to know thee who alone art truly God, and Jesus Christ whom thou hast sent" (John 17: 3).

I want us to approach our subject parallel to that outlined by the Everest Leader in *Ascent of Everest*. This book will become a parable for Christian endeavour and experience.

Sir John Hunt writes that it is well over thirty years since the first expedition was sent to explore the mountain. Since then no less than eleven major expeditions have followed. The ascent of Everest was not the work of one day, nor of a few anxious unforgettable weeks, but a protracted attempt over a long period of time and of tenacious endeavour.

The ascent of the Inner Everest has been a challenge to man since the beginning. Fallen man has sought continually to climb it. In the East five hundred million souls pursue the gentle and peaceful religion of Buddhism. Gautama was twenty-nine years of age when he left his beautiful wife and child to solve the riddle of life. By mortification, meditation and starvation he pursued the solution for six years, but confessed to failure. Then came forty-nine days of meditation at Bodh Gaya. He claimed enlightenment. He preached for forty-five years the four great Truths. His last words were, "Work out your own salvation with diligence." His proposed way to the Summit was by personal renunciation and diligence.

Another three hundred and fifty million men and women follow the simplest of religious dogma, but the most complex in practice. For the essence of Hinduism is pure but its practice gross. The doctrine puzzles the West. Its objective is but to attain unity with the eternal Spirit — a sacred Brahm or "Om". This is their Absolute and Ultimate. Its path is mysterious, illimitable and ineffable. In one epic alone, the Mahabharata, the attempt to describe its way is in volume three times greater than that of our own Bible. Their way up is by non-violence, purity, self-control, charity and compassion.

The seed of Confucian thought lies buried, but not dead, in the hearts of almost six hundred million Chinese. It awaits a climax to blossom. For them light and darkness are elements not in opposition, but in accord and harmony. The way to the Ultimate is "Tao" — a way, a road. Leave things alone, for all will settle themselves. What is contrary to Tao must finally cease. Only true Tao will remain. Man is essentially good and cannot but surely reach his summit — so let alone.

Thus by personal disciplines and self-resources one thousand four hundred million souls seek to conquer their Inner Everest and attain the Ultimate Reality, the Essential Self, the Infinite Harmony.

Out of Judaism comes the cry, "Oh, that I might know Him." This is the cry of millions of souls over years of expeditionary experience to be one with the Ultimate, the Absolute, with God.

Let us now take the Guide Book, the Bible, and turn to the first section. I find that God, at the moment of the failure of His creation, gave the promise of a Saviour — a Guide. God speaks to Satan, "And I will put enmity between thee and the woman, and between thy seed and her seed; it shall bruise thy head, and thou shalt bruise his heel" (Gen. 3: 15). Satan's defeat by the victorious suffering Christ is foretold so that man may regain the fellowship with God that he lost. Can you lift

13

yourself by your shoe laces? No more will you ascend one foot of your Everest by your own human resources.

You and I need help from another Source. This is a basic truth which must be clearly seen and then implemented in our daily walk. No one can ignore this lesson. The first Adam flunked his examination. The last Adam passed with an honours degree. You and I cannot escape coming to grips with this issue. The Lord testifies to His need of external spiritual help when He said, "I can of mine own self do nothing" (John 5: 30). Again He says "The words that I speak unto you I speak not of myself: but the Father that dwelleth in me, he doeth the works" (John 14: 10).

The Apostle Paul wrote expansively of this great truth. A choice extract is from his letter to the Galatians, "I have been crucified with Christ: the life I now live is not my life, but the life which Christ lives in me; and my present bodily life is lived by faith in the Son of God, who loved me and gave himself up for me" (Gal. 2: 20).

F. S. Smythe writes in *Everest 1933* of his astounding climb above Camp VI at 27,000 ft. After leaving Eric Shipton, who was unable to climb another step, Smythe says he was so conscious of another "presence" climbing with him. It was friendly and seemed to sustain him in strength. The "presence" was so real that when he ate his morning snack of mint cake he divided it in half and turned instinctively to offer it to his companion! Oh, to know our Source of strength so intimately. This could almost be a spiritual testimony of anyone beginning to climb their Inner Everest. I am "roped" to One who will never leave me. Jesus, who by His death and resurrection spanned the great crevasse, promises to

14

lead me higher up the mountain on a summit assault.

Thus the route to the top is forced and the mountain made "to go". Hallelujah!

Sadhu Sundar Singh crossed the Himalayas time and time again as a Christian missionary to Tibet. In 1929 he failed to return to India. Somewhere in Tibet he laid down his life. Let me share how this fanatical Sikh discovered his Climbing Companion of both physical and spiritual altitudes.

In 1903, as a boy of 14 and a bitter opponent of Christianity, he burnt a Bible — but life already held nothing for him in any fulfilment and purpose. He planned suicide at Ranpur by lying in front of the Lahore express at 5 a.m. — unless God revealed Himself some way, somehow. Listen to his own words. "O God, if there be a God, reveal Thyself before I die." The hours passed. Outside the moon rose clear and white in the winter sky; a pair of jackals raced past the house screaming in the still air. The howl of a hyena broke the silence, but he scarcely heard them. He sat motionless on the floor sensing only an endless drumming of express wheels in his mind.

The moon swung across the sky.

At about quarter to five his room was filled with light. No, it was no trick of the moon, for out of the brightness he saw the Lord Jesus Christ approach and speak to him in wondrous tones of love. "Sundar, how long will you persecute Me? I have come to save you. You were praying to know the right way. Why do you not take it? I am the Way." Sadhu Sundar Singh continued, "He spoke in Hindustani, He spoke to me. I fell at His feet — I cannot say how long I knelt. As I finally rose the brightness faded. Till the day I die my life is His."

15

So any success on the Inner Everest will not come from human resources, no matter how moral and sincere they may appear to be. The ascent is only in following the steps of Another; being linked with Him in inward communion; drawing continually spiritual power and enabling and committing myself in unquestioning obedience to the Lord Jesus Christ. Are you prepared to "rope up" to this Saviour Companion?

2

The Problems

"WHAT is the problem of Everest?" asks Sir John Hunt. "What were the weapons with which the mountain has so long succeeded in holding at bay so many resolute men?" He answered that there were three awe-inspiring factors — altitude, climate and terrain. The lack of oxygen in the one, the uncertainty of the next, and the experience and skill demanded by the last.

The problems are identical when we consider our Inner Everest. There is a lack, an uncertainty, and a demand upon the climbers.

Problem No. 1 The life breath at altitudes is oxygen. It maintains life and sustains energy. Its absence promotes cyanosis, harbours toxins and accelerates disease. Men slumping into the coma of the death-sleep of the snows have been revived with a few whiffs of oxygen, and later, with its aid have descended without a companion to lower camps. The spiritual mountaineer of the Inner Everest will never make an ascent without the Holy Breath of God. It is his life and health and peace. The Psalmist confirms this as he writes, "That thy way may be known upon earth, thy saving health among all nations" (Psa. 67: 2). Sleep at 27,000 ft. above sea level without oxygen is a shallow subconsciousness punctuated by dreams and irregular breathing. Oxygen used later by the 1958 expedition gave the climbers the needed restful invigorating sleep. Men, unaided by God's

Holy Breath-Spirit, know only a shallow conscious-ness of life torn by fears, apprehensions, convictions and the pressures of condemnation. "There is no peace, saith my God, to the wicked" (Isa. 57: 21). "Now if any man have not the Spirit of Christ, he is none of his" (Rom. 8: 9). Thus this initial problem for the unregenerate man is one of deficiency, and lack of the breath of spiritual life; the lack of a "born again" experience.

To be "born again" is a term I feel is far too loosely used in terms of spiritual experience. Its origin is found in Jesus Christ's reply to Nicodemus (John 3: 7). Jesus meant that man must find new life in Him. I expect this new life of Christ to be a vital revolution of a man's whole outlook. Am I asking too much to expect a "born again" person to find the reading of God's Word an essential and enriching practice; that he or she will want friendships with others who love the Lord? I would expect to see them at prayer meetings of Christian fellowship. I cannot equate a "born again" person finding Christ the centre and be-all of life continuing with worldly friendships, fashions that prejudice modesty, music and magazines stimulating sex. It just does not add up straight. New life is new life, not the old life under a new name.

While in Australia in 1969 I had an enjoyable, stimulating, although very full weekend at a Youth Centre. On Saturday afternoon a fine young man sat with me in my room. His problem was that the Christian life was not worth it! He said he was a Christian, and he wanted to follow Christ. But why should he have to give up so much? His pals in the world had sex three times a week; why couldn't he? I don't apologise for taking the lid off life. These are the battles and problems of young Christians today in a world of no moral standards in society. I opened the "Guide Book" and we faced what Jesus demanded for new life in Him. It was His life for ours. Nothing more and nothing less. The young man left my room sad and unwilling. As my car swung out of the Youth Centre he ran up radiant — "It's all over! I'm His! No problems now."

Problem No. 2 Now let us face the second problem of uncertainty. For Sir John Hunt it was the uncertainty of the weather. He said that the chance to get up Everest is probably limited to the lull between the fury of the winter's gales and the onset of the warm damp wind from the Bay of Bengal. It was the uncertainty of climate. The man who climbs but a little distance up his Inner Everest is soon most conscious of the storm passions of sin and self. He is beaten back numbed and disheartened again and again. Moral standards alone linked with high endeavour make no progress against the lashing winds of temper and lust. Man would wish it otherwise, but it is impossible. What hope is there for the unregenerate when even that doughty mountaineer, Paul, exclaims in his disappointment and failure, "I am unspiritual, the purchased slave of sin. I do not even acknowledge my own actions as mine, for what I do is not what I want to do, but what I detest" (Rom. 7: 14, 15)? This is the outburst of a beaten, exhausted climber overcome by the uncertainty of the climate of his sin and self. Thank God he became "a summitter". Therefore we can take heart even though so conscious of the falls, slips and flounderings that cancel out any progress and sometimes seem to put our very presence on the mountain in jeopardy. This problem is very real to many Christians. It is a problem that faces the young and old alike. It is a problem only answered when Christ effectively "ropes" Himself to me that my progress might be safe and steady. He calls to me across the dangers and uncertainties of life, "I will never, never, never, never, never forsake you" (Dr Babbage of Melbourne, exposition of Joshua 1.5).

The joy and thrill of my life in Christ is that it is a victorious life. The terrible cost of the Cross could have bought nothing less for me and for all. I could never hide a defeated dissatisfied Christian life under a rationalising testimony that Christ's life and victory is only *imputed* to me. The Scripture is clear that this life is *given* me. "If a man loves me, he will keep my word, and my Father will love him, and we will come to him and make our home with him" (John 14: 23). I have discovered this to be true in the experimental test tube of Christian life.

*   *   *

My wife and I climbed the frail ladder to the platform of a house in Thailand. About thirty sat around the room against the wall. Most of these dear souls were only about two years old spiritually. The Bible was opened and the leader began to read. Hardly had he covered two or three verses than he was interrupted by a woman opposite who begged to give word of testimony of what Jesus had meant to her last week. This was followed by a few further verses and a further interruption! A brother in the Lord unburdened his heart of what Christ meant to him. Then the reading continued, only to be further interrupted. Another woman poured out her heart of the goodness and love of her Saviour. The leader realising the truth of the old maxim, "If you cannot

20

beat them, then join them", ventured his own testimony!

Family feuds are real in Thailand, sometimes whole families being wiped out. That week this leader had been shot at but was unharmed. He chased his assailant, not to kill him, but to share Christ with him. The man got away. "This morning," the leader continued, "I turned the corner and bumped into him. I held him fast and shared with him my love for him and his family. He need have no fear of us. I told him of Christ who has changed our lives. Pray for him; he may be here next week." I looked around at these Thai believers — redeemed drunkards, opium addicts, and potential murderers, now climbing high by God's grace, love and indwelling Presence.

Problem No. 3 Everest demands experience and skill to combat the terrain. Those who followed the accounts of earlier expeditions assaulting the mountain from Tibet and the Rongbuk glacier know how continually the climbers referred to "the slabs", the "first band" and the "second band". The slabs were smooth outwardly sloping rocks. The only grip was the friction of a nailhead of one's boots. The "bands" demanded rock climbing skill; although not even difficult to climb if but a few thousand feet above sea level, they demanded the resources of a superman on top of the world at 28,000 ft. "The peak of Everest would demand an undistracted mind as well as a reserve of strength," writes Sir John. "This was the supreme question to whose solution the whole of our planning was ultimately directed." Now listen to the Great Guide: "If anyone wishes to be a follower of mine, he must leave self behind; day after day he must take up his

21

cross, and come with me. Whoever cares for his own safety is lost; but if a man will let himself be lost for my sake, that man is safe. Another said, 'I will follow you, sir; but let me first say goodbye to my people at home.' To him Jesus said, 'No one who sets his hand to the plough and then keeps looking back is fit for the kingdom of God' " (Luke 9: 23–27, 61, 62). All the experience required for the ascent of our Inner Everest is lodged in our Guide. We are nothing, we know nothing and we can do nothing. The sooner we realise this, the better the problem is understood. Our Divine Guide asks of us but one thing — implicit and continual obedience. The Bible is often called a Textbook. Should that be so then it tells me of my relationship with the problem and how to deal with it. Is it not also true to say that the Bible is a Test Book? I am continually challenged to a new relationship with my Lord — my Guide, in doing what He tells me to do. The Lord will continually demand of me steps of faith and stances of obedience.

*   *   *

I opened a large envelope bearing Indian stamps and out fell a few photographs and a new slim hymn-book written in a hill dialect. They were all connected with a new church deep in the Himalaya. My mind went back sixteen years.

The Indian Government had given orders that all aliens were to move back over fifty miles from the Tibetan Border and a corridor of a prohibited defence zone was formed. This order drastically curtailed our work. The main issue was whom we should ask to carry on. It would need to be an Indian national, either person or organisation.

22

A young South Indian student of the Yeotmal Seminary sat in our Conference that year. His coming to us was a thrilling answer to prayer. We listened to his testimony. Born a Hindu of a father who was a renowned Brahmin priest of a well known temple. Won by the love of the Lord Jesus Christ, he suffered persecution and was put out of his home. Daily he prayed until the whole family and his father were converted.

A deep desire to follow Jesus more adequately led him to seminary training. During his last term God laid on A. K. George's heart a desire to work where western missionaries could not go. That was why he was with us. Fresh-faced and eager in Spirit he felt God's hand on him. We held back from handing the work over to him until he had travelled to this remote area to see for himself.

He had been gone over two weeks when suddenly I met him in the bazaar at Mussoorie, North India. He was thin, pale, ill, with clothes dirty and torn. In no time he was admitted to the Community Hospital. I well remember saying to myself that this was the end of our hopes in "A. K."

I sat beside the bed to listen to his story. For a young man from equatorial banana groves to travel to ice-bound Himalayan fastnesses was as big a decision to make as for any western missionary to leave homeland and sail to foreign shores. His experiences were very real and demanding upon him physically and spiritually. I ventured the question. "Well, 'A. K.', I suppose we must be prepared for your decision against returning." He turned a radiant smile to me. "Not to go back ! God has called me. This is His will. I *must* go back."

For sixteen years he has laboured with others joining him from South India. Believers have been baptised and it appears a church of some twenty members bears witness and testimony to Christ. Western missionaries had laboured for seventy years and seen but a few souls. But we had ploughed and sown. God by His Spirit waters. "A. K." was given the joy to begin reaping. But behind all this lies a decision of sacrificial obedience. He has left his wife and family for three-year periods, returning for six months' furlough, after which he faces the border again — all for Jesus' sake.

"A. K." climbs high upon his Inner Everest. Simply following the Lord obediently — whatever the cost.

When the judgment day of believers dawns I shall feel my own years of service to be without comparison to such as "A. K." His name will be high on the Divine Honours Roll.

Our inadequacy, the uncertainties of life and the demands of God are the problems of the Inner Everest. These are the Supreme Questions for which God has made adequate and overwhelming provision in His Divine Plan of Assault.

3

The Climbers

MY INNER EVEREST is a very personal climb, shared only with my relationship with the Lord. But the summit is not reached on my own. I was never intended to climb alone. This is not a contradiction of the first statement. Do remember how Paul tried to hammer this home to the Corinthian fellowship, "The body (of Christ) is not one member, but many" (1 Cor. 12: 14). "Now you are the body of Christ and individually members of it" (1 Cor. 12: 27).

Christ is ministered to me by His living in and through others. We need each other, and often we are desperately in need of each other! Tragedy always seems to accompany the man or woman who feels independently sufficient in spiritual things. Lack of balance in spiritual truths and wrong emphasis usually results in "going it alone". My spiritual life is helped and enriched and guarded by my fellow climbers in the Lord. God uses others to reveal much within me needing to be dealt with. I am disciplined by another shoulder rubbing mine in the daily routine, or by one to whom I am roped on this climb. Although Sir John Hunt knew that there would only be "one summit pair", they needed twelve others to get them to the top. Each of us needs the fellowship of others in our personal ascent. We cannot choose our party. God chooses them for us. He will not fail to pick the right men and women! This is a test whether I really do believe in the sovereignty of God in my life or not. If I do believe this then I must accept the most uncongenial member of the party as the Lord's wise choice for me. As Jesus picks His men for us, we find we also have our Peters, Jameses and Philips. Look at the party our Lord chose Himself for the training of each disciple and I shall find it is truly reflected in the ones He has chosen for me. I am sure these following cameos will picture men and women I know and touch day by day.

Peter In all the lists his name comes first. He is that kind of man — impetuous to speak and act. A born leader and a Galilean. Josephus was for a time the Governor of Galilee and so knew them that he wrote, "They are always full of innovations and disposed to changes. They delight in seditions. They would willingly follow a leader into an insurrection. Galileans are notoriously quarrelsome and quick tempered, but with all that they are the most chivalrous of men, and full of courage." Peter was a Galilean to the core.

Andrew Introduced as Simon Peter's brother. Some people are introduced in this manner, persons who are never to the forefront, but usually overshadowed by some others. In the account given by John the disciple, we find him emerging and revealing a personality which introduces others to Christ. He always appeared to want to be near Jesus. He did not want credit but was always prepared graciously to take second place.

James One of the inner circle. A very impulsive, quick-tempered man. His violent blazing-out gained him the name "son of thunder." He was also a very ambitious man, always desiring a place where the final decisions were made in their affairs.

John His personal portrait in the Gospels is not a beautiful one. Third of the inner three disciples, he was a young man insisting on everyone else toeing the line. He was prepared to call down fire on those who did not conform to his wishes! He had a hot temper and intolerant heart. Yet, Jesus made him the Apostle of love.

Philip He was the first disciple to be called by Jesus, and he showed a determination to share Christ with others. A fine personal worker who would not get drawn into an argument, but just said, "Come and see." He was warm-hearted, but a bit pessimistic. He did not like responsibility, but was wise in referring matters to others who were more able.

Bartholomew (Nathaniel) Philip's friend and an honest sceptic. There could be no duplicity or cunning about him. He hated deception like the plague. a man in whom there is no guile

Thomas A courageous man, often bewildered! He had devotion and faith, but spoilt it by being gloomy and very pessimistic. He always wanted to make sure first, and continually put the brake on affairs.

Matthew Being a tax-gatherer, he was the most hated and despised of men. Stapfer called tax-gatherers "a class of despised pariahs". His clan were linked by the Jews with adulterers and informers, murderers and robbers. They would be the Quislings of our present day. But Matthew by reason of his vocation was able to write, and most likely was the first man to present to the world in literature the teachings of Jesus.

James (the Less) A fiery patriot, probably the bane of his placid colleague Andrew.

Lebbaeus A violent nationalist. He is only once mentioned, and then he is pressing Jesus to declare Himself as the Liberator. Jesus' reply was to reveal the only loyalty worthwhile — that of a loving heart.

Simon the Zealot Nothing is told us of him — only his name! And Zealot tells us everything! He is one of those heroic fanatics who would use all and every violence to attain an end.

Judas The odd man out by not being a Galilean, and thereby was not fully understood by the others. He held an important job and sat in a place of honour. He was not of the inner three.

So this is the party that Jesus chose and which surrounded Him for three years. Upon them the imprint of the Lord's personality became so marked that we find them spending days together in the upper room awaiting the coming of the Holy Spirit. They became men of prayer and the Word and above all became men of obedience.

They surround us today. Do we not see the "grace" of Andrew tempering the "fire" of the four nationalists; and pessimism chafing against impetuosity; patriots against a national pariah and traitor; meticulous Philip getting the victory over impetuous John? Surely there should have been a murder, continual quarrelling, a resignation and two splits. No two of them could have worked on the same Mission station or on the same church diaconate together.

Jesus prayed, "That they may be one, even as we are one" (John 17:22). Several of them reached high camps on the Inner Everest. Do we now see why God has chosen the men and women we are to be roped with at various levels of life? No matter how impossible it may appear for us all to be able to climb together, a day will surely come when the whole unlikely crowd of us will be "of one accord in one place".

It is hard to analyse oneself accurately, but I imagine as a young man I had a lot of Peter's personality about me. Impetuous and so often irresponsible. Then the day came when I entered a training college for overseas missionary service. I might have been my church's blue-eyed boy, but amongst twenty other men I was cut down to size — and very quickly at that. There was another at the college who "got my back up". It took all I had not to give him a "broadside" of my feelings. He was so slow, indecisive, with several other characteristics that rubbed me continually. I got through two terms by steering clear of him.

Arriving at the opening of the third term of my first year I looked at the accommodation list to find, to my horror, that I was to share a room with this paragon of provocation. I dared not ask for a switch. I just knew I had to accept it and all that came with it.

That night I saw in my colleague a different person. He was a man of prayer. He loved to read the Word. These two aspects of Christian discipline and devotion I seriously lacked. Within the week I was hungry to possess such a relationship with the Lord. To cut a longer story short let it be said that I was deeply enriched by his spiritual life. I needed him in my weakness. Because I needed him I wanted him. Because I wanted him all other previous repelling factors faded into insignificance. Bless God for putting me with this dear man that term.

This is the basic spiritual truth. God gave His gifts to each of us. He did not give all His gifts to one — thank God. And the Scripture says the premise for the distributed spiritual ministries is that we all may profit. "To each is given the manifestation of the Spirit for the common good" (1 Cor. 12: 7).

So you and I have three courses open to us in relation to a difficult climbing colleague. One — we can avoid him like the plague. With the least contact the least provocation! Or two, we can grit our teeth and pray for grace to "grease" the friction points! Or lastly, we can see in the other the graces and gifts of God we each so sorely need to enrich our lives. We always see what we look for, by the way, so do not say there are no positive spiritual factors about him or her. They are there. Ask God to show you them. Then open your life to their influence and your arms to their fellowship. This is the path of victory. This is why God never planned for me to climb alone.

His promises are always to a fellowship. "Where two or three are gathered together in my name, there am I in the midst of them" (Matt. 18: 20). "If two of you shall agree on earth as touching anything that they shall ask, it shall be done for them of my Father which is in heaven" (Matt. 18: 19). "Two are better than one . . . because, if one falls, the other can help his companion up again; but alas for the man who falls alone with no partner to help him up" (Eccles. 4: 9).

Who, now, would climb alone?

4

The Equipment

THE EARS of St. Paul grew accustomed to news of the arena contests, so it became natural for him to liken the Christian soldier to the gladiator (Eph. 6: 10–18). Similarly today it becomes a newspaper scoop to get the first details of a climb on the north face of the Eiger, or the exclusive rights to a mountaineering expedition leaving to attack a Himalayan giant. I am sure Paul, if he lived today, would have made the mountaineer parabolic to the Christian life. So let us therefore clothe our mountaineer with spiritual equipment.

The Rope This can easily be equated with the belt of the Christian soldier in Eph. 6: 14, "Take your stand then with truth as your belt." Not only does it assure the safety of each climber on the rope but it is wrapped around each man at the waist. We could paraphrase and adapt this verse as follows: "Stand therefore having tightened the rope of truth around your waist," and also Psa. 91: 4, "His truth shall be thy shield and buckler," to "His truth shall be thy rope."

Truth is the eternity of God in the certainty of His character, purpose and will for my life. The Truth of God *is* my safety. The rope is always used when in danger of a slip, both for one's own personal safety and for the security of the team. Steep and difficult pitches in ascent or descent demand its use to safeguard lives. The rope is always tied to another climber, or to a rock holdfast for a firm anchorage.

These are also spiritual truths. In a great measure we hold one another to the highest by the character and presence of Christ in each other's lives. Look at Samuel trying to hold Saul (1 Sam. 15: 22). Nathan anchors David in that dangerous fall (2 Sam. 12: 11–14). Agabus and the disciples deeply concerned about the safety of Paul (Acts 21: 4, 10). Paul struggles to secure the Corinthian Church in their exposed position (2 Cor. 13: 1–4).

Again we are anchored by His truth to the Rock Christ Jesus. It is the safeguard in our ascent into revival and blessing against human pride and confidence in the flesh. It is the safeguard in vision and commission against a sense of personal ability to "put it through". It is our security in descent. Often there are short periods of descent across a col or saddle even when proceeding to the summit. True again in the Christian ascent, for we leave points of blessing for the valley of the shadow. Did not our Lord descend to where He could say, "This is *your* hour, and the power of darkness" (Luke 22: 53)? The rope of truth assures us in our trudge through the heaviness of sorrow and grief (Isa. 53: 3). Truth holds us and steadies us *through it* — note that it does *not save us from it* (John 12: 27, Luke 22: 28). How often those that anxiously watch the climber are in doubt and uncertainty of the situation, while the climber himself, feeling the tautness of the rope of truth, knows security.

The Goggles These yellow tinted glasses in a protective frame filter out the sight-destroying rays which are so potent at high altitudes. This condition is exaggerated by the reflected glare off the pure white snow. The coloured lens is a shield and also a corrective for the eyesight. I can see a proper image without strain and distortion. Remove my snow-goggles in such conditions and I am a casualty. Paul likened such a shield in Eph. 6: 16 to our faith. This spiritual weapon is both protective and corrective. Without it the destroying factors of unbelief and criticism rob me of my faculty to see clearly and in perspective. I cannot see clearly or walk confidently. I am unable to gauge and decide upon a route. Immediately I slip my goggles of faith over my eyes I see, walk, climb and pick my route without doubt.

Not only is my own progress marked with confidence, but my relationship with others is also vitally improved. Naturally we experience difficulty in working in harmony with others. We "see" weaknesses and immaturity which thereby promote mistrust and create feelings. F. S. Smythe writes of the anger and antagonism which he felt towards another climber only because of the clumsy, inefficient way he kicked the steps in the snow. Yet when Smythe himself took over the lead he was just as clumsy and boggled his steps. Every Christian knows the parallel truth of intolerance and criticism we feel in watching other Christians at work. If you do not believe me, then attend an average church business meeting! But this is life in the flesh, *not* in the Spirit. The Lord said a great truth when it is recorded, "Blessed are the pure in heart: for they shall see God" (Matt. 5: 8). I do not take this to mean only that one day I *shall* see God, but, being pure in heart *now*, I see God *now*. I see Him in others, in their work, in their fellowship. The goggles of faith reveal to me the presence of Jesus. I see others framed in the grace of God. How else could Paul write in his letter to the Corinthian Church,

"Believe all things, hope all things — Love never fails" (1 Cor. 13: 7, 8).

There is a classic example of this in the historical record of the children of Israel in Joshua 22. There had been wonderful unity in the nation as they fought for their inheritance. Victory brought the day when they could enjoy the fruits of their victory. It also released the two-and-a-half tribes to return to their homes east of Jordan. They had fulfilled their vow.

Then something happened. These two-and-a-half tribes built a great altar, and built it in a very provocative place.

The news spread. Rumours became facts. The two-and-a-half tribes were accused and judged of leaving the one true God. This was rebellion! They were instituting a rival holy place, a separate worship. Of course, it is only a small step to bring spiritual reasons to bear upon the issue and make the reaction one of "defending the faith". This sin, of course, was against God. They quoted precedents such as Achan's sin. This was a true case for a holy war. Israel was mobilised.

But the two-and-a-half tribes desired to explain, and a good job they did so. This is their defence. They were greatly exercised about their children growing up far away from the Holy City. They had no symbol nor reminder. Distance could estrange them from the God of Israel. "We are not rebellious. Our desire is for our children to continue in the knowledge of the God of Israel."

The armies are disbanded. The explanation is accepted and even lauded. The altar shall remain as a symbol and reminder. Everyone is happy. But it was a near thing.

If only enquiry and concern were first expressed instead of judgment and armed mobilisation.

As Field Leader of a W.E.C. Fellowship in the Himalayas I learnt to my cost never to read a letter apart from the "goggles of faith". Suspicion and the negative interpretation of the ambiguous always destroyed trusted bonds of fellowship. I had got into a habit of reading "between the lines" with the inevitable consequences. These proven "goggles of faith" correct this deflection and bring the eyesight on to the line. It was a bitter lesson for me to learn. But God is so gracious in His chastisement. I find it a thrill today to live believing in others as I want others to believe in Christ's work in me. They do not trust me — but Christ in me. As the lens of faith covers my sight, Christ focuses into clear perspective. It makes me to "believe all things and hope all things," permitting nothing to come between my Lord and myself and my fellow climbers.

The Boots "And having shod your feet . . . with the firm-footed stability, (which is) the readiness produced by the good news of the gospel of peace" (Eph. 6: 15).

Translators all confess to difficulty in translating this verse, but one possible meaning comes through the often used "implied sense" of the Septuagint version. "Shod with the basis (footing) of the Gospel of Peace." We can stand on no other conviction or security than on peace. The Gospel is a declaration of peace. My heart should have no other rule than that of peace (Col. 3: 15). My personal life must be based on peace, and my companionship with another is to be strong in a peaceful fellowship. My faith must be anchored in the

35

Scriptural promises that I know can bring peace to any who trust in Him.

The Ice Axe It is a two-edged (adze and point) weapon even as is the sword. Note in Eph. 6: 17 we are "to take," which means "accept" or "receive". It does not become a part of me such as a characteristic, but it is a function of God. We are told it is the Word of God. The Greek original shows it to be the "spoken" word of God. The Gospel of Christ wherever and however it "goes out" defeats evil in all its stratagems.

The mountaineer uses the ice axe in many ways, but usually with three purposes. First, to cut steps to aid ascent of a steep slope. Second, to help in balance when crossing a traverse or a steep slope. Third, by plunging the axe-shaft to its blade in the snow to make it an anchorage for the rope. The Word of God has exactly these three activities. By its promises we move higher and higher against apparently impossible difficulties. In places of bewilderment where blow the winds of many doctrines and interpretations of Truth, it is only the Word that can maintain our balance and poise. Not just a dipping into the Scriptures as and when we feel a need, but the continual reading and re-reading that anchors us in the Living Word. Recently I was at a morning fellowship of full-time Christian workers who are members of the West Croydon Tabernacle. Mr. Quinton Carr, of the Scripture Union, shared with us the results of a recent enquiry among Christians concerning regular daily reading of the Scriptures. It appears, from these results, that about sixty per cent of Christians do **not** read the Scriptures daily in any systematic manner whatsoever! Paul underlines the necessity of wearing the armour and being conversant with the weapons, that are the Word of God. The same is true in the analogy of our climber. To lose an ice axe on Everest is a tragedy, and places the climber in a very, very dangerous position. Oh, that Christians would also realise the personal danger and tragedy when they act as if the Word of God is not relevant to life.

After speaking at a young people's meeting I was asked to help a young lady who had lost the joy of the Christian life and did not know why or where her former thrill of living for Christ lifted from her. I noticed she wore an engagement ring and asked about her fiancé. Very embarrassed she shared that he was not a Christian, but she felt that her friendship and marriage would lead him to the Lord. I pressed the question concerning her regular Bible reading to find the Word was only opened at the meetings she attended.

Gently I shared that she had lost her joy because of her ignorance and thereby her disobedience to the basic premise of Christian living as clearly stated in the Word. "What premise? What basic have I disobeyed?" she asked in sincere defence. Turning to 2 Cor. 6: 14, I asked her to read aloud. "Do not unite yourselves with unbelievers; they are no fit mates for you." After a quiet pause I said, "Your joy will return in obedience." The Truth of the Word would hold her from tragedy. Faith would enable her to see, without the distortion of emotion and deep affectionate feelings, the clear-cut position she must take up. The continual reading of the Bible regularly, and daily implementing its principles, safeguards our position at any altitude.

5

The Morale

ONE THING more is required in addition to the essential items of equipment. Sir John Hunt calls it "morale". Morale is the elimination of all that is fearful and uncertain.

The word "morale" lies at the very heart of the story of Gideon in the verses 1–7 of Judges, chapter 7. In fact, that word sums up the whole matter. It was the elimination of everyone who was fearful and trembling, and of those who could contribute to a defeat. This was a great reducing movement by the Lord to obtain a certain quality in His army. Numbers have nothing to do with morale, or the final result. It is completely immaterial to God to save by many or by a few (1 Sam. 14: 6).

Field Marshal Sir William Slim was my Divisional General and Commander during the war. He says that this "morale is a state of mind; it is that intangible force which will move a whole group of men to give their last ounce of strength to achieve some objective without counting the cost to themselves."

In analysis morale has a spiritual, intellectual and material composition. The spiritual must come first in priority, as only spiritual men can take the strain. The intellectual factor is important because men are swayed by reason as well as by their feelings. The material is last, but not least, because the highest morale is often when the material conditions are the worst.

The Spiritual Basis of morale says it must be a great and noble objective. We find the answer to the spiritual mountaineer's question in Phil. 3: 10, "That I may know him, and the power of his resurrection, and the fellowship of his sufferings, being made conformable unto his death." Not only a noble objective, but also its achievement must be vital. "Not as though I had already attained, either were already perfect: but I follow after, if that I may apprehend (grasp) that for which also I am apprehended (grasped or held)" (Phil. 3: 12).

The method of its achievement must be active and aggressive. "But this one thing I do, forgetting those things which are behind, and reaching forth unto those things which are before, I press toward the mark for the prize . . ." (Phil. 3: 13, 14).

A person must be sure that what he is and what he does is directly contributing towards this objective. "Likewise the Spirit also helpeth our infirmities: for we know not what we should pray for as we ought: but the Spirit itself maketh intercession for us with groanings which cannot be uttered" (Rom. 8: 26).

The Intellectual Basis of morale demands that a man is convinced that the objective is attainable. Nothing stimulates faith more than to see the blueprint of objectives and to be assured of the resources available. This the Apostle Paul dramatically portrays in the first chapter of his letter to the church in Ephesus. To read these opening declarations is like looking over the shoulder of an architect-draughtsman drawing out the plans and elevations of a new edifice. Then the architect writes in the resources and authority to build. It is stimulating. "The eyes of your understanding being enlightened; that ye may know what is the hope of his calling, and what

39

the riches of the glory of his inheritance in the saints . . . and hath put all things under his feet" (Eph. 1: 18, 22).

A man must likewise be convinced that the organisation to which he belongs is sound and efficient. This is also assured us by the Holy Spirit. "Now therefore ye . . . are built upon the foundation of the apostles and prophets, Jesus Christ himself being the chief corner stone . . . an habitation of God through the Spirit" (Eph. 2: 19–22).

A man must finally be convinced of the ability and competence of his leaders in spite of hardship and death. Can the Scriptures more strongly assure us than this testimony: "For if we be dead with him, we shall also live with him: if we suffer, we shall also reign with him" (2 Tim. 2: 11, 12)?

The Material Basis demands that a man feels he is getting a square deal from his leader and team.

The line of temptation often may come along the line of feeling a task has been given beyond one's capabilities and strength. At times indignation may begin to smoulder when feeling we are not being dealt with fairly. These thoughts are unworthy of our Lord and Master. Yet this assurance is often blurred when we look at His servants whom He is using in our circumstances. We must look at the signature on the letter, not at the postman! "He (Jesus) said unto me, My grace is sufficient for thee: for my strength is made perfect in weakness. Most gladly therefore will I glory in my infirmities, that the power of Christ may rest upon me" (2 Cor. 12: 9).

A man must be given the best of equipment. In Christ the finest possible makes up our kit list. "Finally, my brethren . . . put on the whole armour of God" (Eph. 6: 10, 11).

A man must feel his conditions are made as good as possible. The question that keeps annoying and disturbing is whether my leader knows with what conditions I am having to cope. Paul settled this once and for all in this testimony: "I have learned, in whatsoever state I am, therewith to be content. I know both how to be abased, and I know how to abound: every where and in all things . . . I can do all things through Christ which strengtheneth me" (Phil. 4: 11–13).

It was against the possibility of a breakdown in this morale that the Lord took such serious precautions with Gideon and his army. Over ninety-nine per cent of the army was eliminated. A tested hard core of loyal troops remained. "By the three hundred . . . will I save you" (Judges 7: 7). For the ascent of the Inner Everest every climber has the potential of the highest morale possible. He has the best equipment and sovereign grace in all conditions to meet this basic need. It is, of course, all found in Jesus Christ our Lord.

The Battering upon Morale If we pause a moment, we cannot fail to realise what a great deal the New Testament has to say about morale. Look at these entreaties and admonitions: "Be strong in the grace that is in Christ Jesus" (2 Tim. 2: 1); "Be strong in the Lord and in the strength of his might" (Eph. 6: 10); "Quit you like men, be strong!" (1 Cor. 16: 13).

All these have to do with spiritual morale and stamina to keep moving, fighting or climbing. The great objective of the devil is to repudiate the Cause, and one's intelligent understanding of the need, cost and reason for the Cause. In Burma during the last war, for a long time it was impossible to break

41

through the Japanese armies. Sir William Slim told me personally, when I visited him at Government House, Canberra, Australia, that he knew of positions held by 500 Japanese. They had to kill 495 of them, and the remaining five killed themselves! No one would surrender! If everyone had such a confidence and consciousness that this spiritual expedition is for the Highest, that we are in this without reserve or personal interest or pride, and only for the glory of God — then we would constantly live in the victorious presence of Christ and for the triumph of His cause.

Sir John Hunt wanted to give the Conquest of Everest as a coronation gift to Her Majesty Queen Elizabeth. What a gift! This ambition heightened morale. Her Majesty was touched deeply and not ignorant of the cost of such a gift!

The battering of our morale searches out everything that is fearful and trembling. Fear can only mean the presence of other interests and motives. If there is something within me of higher count and greater importance, then that is the source of fear leading to unbelief in my Christian career.

Look again at Gideon's army in Judges 7: 4; "Of whom I say unto thee, This shall go with thee, the same shall go with thee; and of whomsoever I say unto thee, This shall not go with thee, the same shall not go." God dealing with thousands, deals with them personally. The campaign was carried on personal selection. The whole expedition of my Inner Everest is carried on my personal spiritual morale.

The Bonding through Morale My conduct and attitude always affects another who is climbing with me. If my stance and progress is insecure or clumsy;

42

if I keep the rope slack; if I cannot be relied upon in a slip or a fall, then I become the weak link of the team, fellowship or church. That is to say, the way you and I individually stand up to the demands of the ascent affects us all in the end. "None of us liveth to himself, and no man dieth to himself" (Rom. 14: 7).

In the elimination test of Gideon's army, God said in effect that He could not allow any trembling, fearful, unbelieving man to go. Such a one will affect others — this cannot be risked. The army is to be reduced to its sheer basic worth. This, then, explains God's dealing with me in the reducing, emptying, weakening, breaking and shattering experiences I am subjected to in His training. What is God doing? He is making way for the basic values to be revealed in my life when my objective is God alone, and only Him. The issue must solely be His glory, and for His honour.

This is morale. Great issues hang upon it. A lofty summit is to be attained, and the flag of a redemptive ministry *through* me to be planted on its highest point. Nevertheless a powerful enemy is also in the field. The glacier-lassitude of spiritual sloth and laziness will envelop us. Tempted to neglect the equipment and deprecate our climbing companions, we could so easily fail and fall, and in falling pull down another! "Finally, be strong in the Lord and in the strength of his might. Put on the whole armour of God, that you may be able to stand against the wiles of the devil" (Eph. 6: 10, 11). Be strong in the Lord! These principles have been so vital in our missionary fellowship of the Worldwide Evangelization Crusade.

In 1913 C. T. Studd, famous England Test cricketer and missionary to China and India, set sail at fifty-three years of age for the Congo. God gave him the promise as he knelt in his cabin to commend the voyage to God — "This journey is not only for the Sudan, but the whole unevangelised world."

In 1925 God had raised a fellowship of workers already touching Africa, Asia and South America.

In 1930 a great crisis scattered this fellowship until only the one field in Congo and a handful of missionaries were left. He died with the debris of his mission around him. He died with high spiritual morale, breathing his last with "Hallelujah! Hallelujah! Hallelujah!"

In 1970 the W.E.C. reaches out to forty-eight countries with between 800 and 900 missionaries. The indwelling Lord and Christ Jesus is the only true spiritual morale.

6

The Base Camp

THE BASE camp for the Everest assault was right up against the greatest of the obstacles in their path — a massive falling glacier called the "Ice Fall". In fact, breaking into the Western Cwm (pronounced Coom) was dependent on being able to find a way up this great mass of tangled ice. This would be the fulcrum upon which the whole success of the expedition would swing. Thus Base Camp was right up against The Fall.

This starting point was also the anchorage of the expedition. It was the source for the supplies, and the return camp for the injured and sick, a place of convalescence. It was the heart and nerve centre of the life of the expedition. From Base Camp they set out to establish higher bivouacs, yet they could return fairly quickly and safely in event of bad weather or accident. This camp contained all that the expedition needed, and was also the planning point of the entire ascent.

The overshadowing menace of Base Camp on Everest was the Ice Fall. It is just the same in our spiritual ascent. Even at our starting point we face realistically all that the Fall (the sin of Adam) means to any successful ascent into spiritual heights.

The Fall I have been greatly helped in understanding more of this problem through the reading of Norman Grubb's book *God Unlimited*, and much that I share stems from this reading. There is a

45

vital difference between the fall of Lucifer and that of Adam. The name Lucifer means Exalted Being, and was probably the highest of all created beings. In Luke 10: 18 we read, "And he (Jesus) said unto them, I beheld Satan as lightning fall from heaven." In Isa. 14: 13–15 the reason is defined: "For thou hast said in thine heart, I will ascend into heaven, I will exalt my throne above the stars of God: I will sit also upon the mount of the congregation, in the sides of the north: I will ascend above the heights of the clouds; I will be like the most High. Yet thou shalt be brought down to hell, to the sides of the pit."

Ezek. 28: 14–18, "Thou art the anointed cherub that covereth; and I have set thee so: thou wast upon the holy mountain of God; thou hast walked up and down in the midst of the stones of fire. Thou wast perfect in thy ways from the day that thou wast created, till iniquity was found in thee . . . therefore will I cast thee as profane out of the mountain of God: and I will destroy thee, O covering cherub, from the midst of the stones of fire. Thine heart was lifted up because of thy beauty, thou hast corrupted thy wisdom by reason of thy brightness: I will cast thee to the ground, I will lay thee before kings, that they may behold thee. Thou hast defiled thy sanctuaries by the multitude of thine iniquities, by the iniquity of thy traffick; therefore will I bring forth a fire from the midst of thee, it shall devour thee, and I will bring thee to ashes upon the earth in the sight of all them that behold thee."

Satan, before the Fall, was the manifester of Eternal Light, but not that Light himself. He took what Norman Grubb calls a "qualitative" leap or a calculated step which broke open the kingdom of hell. He became its originator, its god, the father of lies and sin-spirit. Satan fixed himself in juxtaposition to God, and thereby fell irrecoverably and beyond redemption. Satan determinedly set himself as rival and alternative to God. His sin is absolute and in totality. He became the god of another dimension.

Adam's fall was qualitative, but not, says Norman Grubb, "calculated", and he shares in *God Unlimited* that it was not in totality. Adam fell through the temptation of another. He did not initiate the situation. He fell through deceit and lies, and also a misrepresentation of God. However, Adam was a responsible being and thereby guilty. He chose to follow a deceiver instead of seeking a way of escape. His fatal interest was the flesh and its attractions rather than revolt against God. If he could, he would have kept both God and his sin. Adam's outlook was not totally reversed. He had not irrecoverably chosen to be evil. He was more kidnapped or shanghaied than a willing devotee of the devil. Adam knew good and evil. Lucifer knows evil as his good. Adam had a moral law, and image of God upon his heart. In Satan that image was obliterated. With Adam after the Fall God could come and talk; he was redeemable.

The Ascent of the Fall We must learn the lesson that Adam failed to learn in the Garden of Eden. This lesson is basic.

The two trees mentioned in Genesis 3 are symbolic. No tree can give either eternal life or everlasting damnation. Eternal Life is a Person, the Spirit of Life. The two trees represent two issues of life, the Divine Triune God and the god of this world.

Life is received and maintained by our tapping the resources provided for us in the Lord Jesus Christ. The analogy of such a receiving is given by the Lord saying we must "eat" and "drink" of His flesh and blood. Such terminology was offensive to the ears of the people of His day. It was made the basis of an accusation of cannibalism within the church. Yet there was no other way to show how the teaching and the Word must become the very life-blood and tissue of our daily living in thought and action. We are constantly pressed to "receive", to take and eat digestively the spiritual food provided.

"Receive ye the Holy Ghost" (John 20: 22); and "as many as received him, to them gave he power to become the sons of God" (John 1: 12). As intelligent beings we must learn how we function. The Garden of Eden was not a place of probation but a classroom of education. Man must act intelligently. God said to Adam "eat" — learn the primary function of receiving. The warning regarding the "tree of the knowledge of good and evil" was part of the education. Man must learn that he can go the wrong way if so tempted. He *must* learn that he was created to live by receiving, that he is a container or vessel only, and can be filled by another spirit. Man had to learn that if he felt a pull in the wrong direction, there was not in him the power to resist. If this is true, then what was he to do when he felt such a pull? There was the Tree of Life — which was Christ in whom is all power to do right and to resist evil.

Adam never so much as glanced in the direction of the Tree of Life. It did not dawn upon him that humans are basically helpless. He had been specifically instructed to eat of *all* the trees in the garden *except* the tree of the knowledge of good and evil. There is no resistance to evil in man but by the Spirit of Truth within him — the fruit of the Tree of Life. Man was created to remain a recipient — nothing

48

more. Adam received the wrong spirit. "And you he made alive, when you were dead through the trespasses and sins in which you once walked, following the course of this world, following the prince of the power of the air, the spirit that is now at work in the sons of disobedience. Among these we all once lived in the passions of our flesh, following the desires of body and mind, and so we were by nature children of wrath, like the rest of mankind" (Eph. 2: 1-3) — the spirit of self-love, the spirit of error.

Man has got to learn the way up the Fall. Our condition is rarely known in reality. Man never does what he pleases, nor does he act in his own strength. Man is always the vehicle of Another. "Greater is he that is in you, than he that is in the world" (1 John 4: 4). Do you see the two *he's*? Sin is not a thing, but a person. If it is not Christ it is —

"another spirit" (2 Cor. 11: 4),

"spirit of anti-Christ" (1 John 4: 3),

"spirit of the world" (1 Cor. 2: 12),

"spirit of fear" (2 Tim. 1: 7),

"spirit of bondage" (Rom. 8: 15).

I *must* learn this basic premise. I cannot of myself do anything. I must recognise that there is a *he* dwelling in me. Jesus had to learn the same lesson — "Though he were a Son, yet learned he obedience by the things which he suffered; and being made perfect . . ." (Heb. 5: 8, 9). Then in John 5: 19 Jesus testifies, "The Son can do nothing of himself"; and again in John 14: 10, "The words that I speak unto you I speak not of myself: but the Father that dwelleth in me, He doeth the works."

I become eternally free and happy when this truth is mine, and this relationship and function is established. Thus the way up the Fall is the way the

Lord went. Paul followed and testified to it when he said to the Galatians: "I am crucified with Christ: nevertheless I live; yet not I, but Christ liveth in me: and the life which I now live in the flesh I live by the faith of the Son of God, who loved me, and gave himself for me" (Gal. 2: 20).

The Saviour has forced the way up the Fall. Hallelujah!

I had been a missionary for some years in India and had not learned this lesson. I had hardly taken a few upward steps of my Inner Everest. Although gratified in such Christian service, I was not honestly satisfied. But God in His gracious way sent along a saintly couple to stay at our headquarters in the Himalayan foothills. We affectionately called them Uncle Frank and Auntie Dulcie.

Saying goodnight, Uncle Frank added, "How about an early walk together to-morrow?" I enthusiastically agreed. I would not have been quite so enthusiastic if I had known what was in store for me. I just thought Uncle Frank wanted me to take him to a vantage point to see the dawn march, in blazing colour, across countless miles of snow ranges.

We walked silently to this vantage point and waited. Uncle Frank said, "Let us sit down." That remark ended any thought of snows at sunrise, for then he went on, "Len, what do you know of Galatians 2: 20?" Without hesitation I replied, "I am crucified with Christ: nevertheless I live; yet not I, but Christ liveth in me: and the life which I now live in the flesh I live by the faith of the Son of God, who loved me, and gave himself for me." He nodded but said, "I did not ask if you could say it — but what you *knew* of it." Another silence . . . "You see, Len, I am so conscious of *you* in the work of the Lord on the Border. When you pray, it is Len

Moules praying. When you speak, it is Len Moules speaking. In your joy, in your planning, it is always Len Moules, not Jesus!" By now I knew a holy searching light was revealing my life and nothing was hid. It was humiliating. "Len, I want you to know Christ living in you — Christ praying, Jesus speaking, the Lord planning, and in all your joy it is Christ rejoicing" . . . silence . . . "Only a crucifixion of your self can release the Lord Jesus Christ to live in and through you, and for you to live by the faith of the Son of God." Uncle Frank quietly rose and left me.

The snows were crimson in the dawn — but I did not see them.

The battle lasted an hour. I capitulated to Christ. Lying on my back on the close-cropped mountain turf, I laid out my arms as if I hung on a cross . . . and prayed, "Lord, I am *now* crucified with you . . . *now*. But I know I live, and this life by faith is your life in me. Lord, be my joy, my ministry, my prayer, my plans."

I rose from the turf knowing I had met with God. Looking back as I write these words I can truly say that my fully committed life in Christ began that morning when Christ committed His life fully to me. I was satisfied at last.

7

The Casualty Station

LET US pick up a remark made very early in the previous chapter about the Base Camp being the place of recuperation and convalescence for the climbers. There are always casualties, and provision must be made for their reception and treatment. As in mountaineering, so in the Christian experience we have breakdowns and tragedy. Referring to actual mountaineering, the casualty list may be under three headings:

1. Failure to take the precautions in wearing snow-goggles and the equipment supplied;

2. Failure to harmonise with the team under severe physiological and psychological conditions;

3. Failure to discipline one's ascent to the acclimatisation of new altitudes. Strained hearts through "rushing" the mountain.

All the above are ruthless in searching out the weaknesses of character and discipline, driving one down again to Base to recover before re-ascent.

There is a spiritual parallel in the ascent of the Inner Everest. Looking around Base Camp we see the all-too-familiar casualties. In fact, we see ourselves. Let us examine this in more detail. Writing in a Christian periodical the Rev. John L. Bird states, "Two years ago the leaders of the Student Missionary Council in America addressed themselves to the cause of the increase of first term failures. A study of the causes and effects, with the case-histories of failures of the mission field, led to the establishment of the one-year plan of the Missionary Council. The plan was designed to give candidates an opportunity to re-adjust their thinking as a result of actual mission field experience.

"In an article in *Moody Monthly* there appeared a tabulation of the causes of missionary failures, and after several years of observation and study it shares with us the possible causes of failure.

"It is on record by those who studied the problems, that the factors of failure were such that they were not noticeable during normal college training. Nor were they evident during the interviews by the Mission Board. So the blame could not be laid on the Council of the College, or upon the Board of the Mission.

"Here then are the causes of failure expressed in percentages. The tabulation is made on the basis of 120 units of failure covering the case history of 100 missionaries. The unit of failure is used because several missionaries had failed on more than one point.

1. Inability to maintain a satisfactory devotional life when isolated from sympathetic believers ... 9%

2. Inability or unwillingness to submit graciously to discipline by the leaders or senior missionary ...16%

3. Inability or unwillingness to work in harmony with another worker 17%

4. Inability to avoid showing superiority to national officials and national workers 17%

5. Inability to maintain happy relations between husband and wife or to be able to conceal such a breakdown. It reflected on to the Mission 9%

6. Inability to prepare accurate and proper financial

accounts, reports, together with slovenliness and evasion of duties 8%

7. Inability to develop a plan of work, to be disciplined in time to a satisfactory routine of life...11%

8. Inability to maintain a standard of cleanliness and personal hygiene, or household tidiness when placed to live in sub-normal conditions 9%

9. Inability to cope with sex problems 4%

"As we examine these figures presented to us from the fourth Annual Missions Conference of Dallas Theological Seminary, it must be noticed that omission has been made of matters where failure has been due to health or scholastic limitations. Failures from these causes are *not* high in proportion to the others.

"The greatest problem of all is that of relationships; lack of discipline, inability to work with others and family stress. These add up to fifty-nine per cent of the casualties.

"The list certainly points emphatically to the need of disciplining one's early life. The results of an undisciplined life at home may clearly be seen on the mission field, but at this later stage they become tragedies.

"Failures due to sex problems were small in number, but their comparative harm was so much greater. The repercussions within the work were far-reaching."

Although Mr. Bird has broken down the causes of casualties into nine groups, I think a re-classification of them will show that they fall into three main areas of failure. It will be seen that these are identical with the reasons shared earlier in the book.

Group A Show failure in their devotional life. They have been found insufficiently protected in the region of their affections. The equipment provided has not been worn.

At our annual conferences of the Tibetan Border Field of the Worldwide Evangelization Crusade, the missionaries came in for fellowship and to seek the spiritual plan for the work during the coming year. Some workers trekked in from lonely stations remote from even normal facilities of a regular postal service. Long before we asked God for guidance on the work, we asked Him to meet us as the workers. Soon the blessed work began as the Spirit prompted confession, apology and personal testimony. I will never forget the broken testimony of a dear fellow worker who had lost out spiritually. The cause — a lust for reading novels. This had displaced the daily Scripture reading and meditation of the Quiet Time. For so many this important time with God is a "hit or miss" experience. They rise from their knees unsatisfied. There could be no question about the time given or the posture taken, but the mind skipped around a thousand thoughts.

Success in a devotional life is linked to a positive practical approach. The Quiet Time should be divided into:

1. A time for worship — thank and praise God in Jesus Christ for what He is in character and work;

2. Follow this with a *systematic reading* of the Word in a day-to-day outline;

3. Then seek the Lord for the requests of the day — these can be included in a prayer list added and adjusted as God burdens you for others, and answers your earlier requests;

4. A period of meditation. Look at the daily programme of people to see, letters to write, counsel to be given, etc. Then reflect how Jesus would write

that letter, counsel the needy, fellowship in the daily contact with others.

Thus refreshed, strengthened and directed, one is prepared for the day.

Group B Inabilities Nos. 2, 3 and 4 show failure in the fellowship. They have been unable to get victory in the mind, or to subjugate themselves in loyalty to others. The uncrucified self has been revealed and at that point has overwhelmed them in the ascent.

I always feel that the place of renewal in the failure of fellowship is in the fellowship! It is so easy to feel discouraged and slink away alone like a sick dog to the cabbage patch. God gave us the fellowship of His Church as the instrument of His spiritual renewing of our lives. We need each other. I have knelt in my own personal need beside another for prayer. I have always stood again in a new dimension of faith and spiritual life. What is more blessed than the loving concern and honest sharing by another who is so able to interpret my need. Thank God for a fellowship with others and with Christ.

It is hard to "break" and confess one's failure and need. But this is the royal road to personal revival. "I dwell in a high and holy place with him who is broken and humble in spirit" (Isa. 57: 15). More often than not it is a lone dealing with God, and the testimony is shared with others afterwards for encouragement and praise to the Lord. Yet, at times the Spirit has led otherwise. In the many years spent at our W.E.C. H.Q. meetings I hold in precious memory the many times God melted us as one and another opened up a heart of need for prayer and spiritual understanding. I know of nothing that heralds personal revival more than the humbling and

56

breaking of my self-spirit before the Lord, and sometimes before the fellowship of His people.

Group C Inabilities 6–9 show failure in discipline and reveal great areas of their lives unevangelised by the Spirit. Although they may be dismissed as insignificant by some, their havoc is great.

The Lord has taught me that this battle is won in the area of the mind. If we fail to inherit God's provision here we are in serious trouble. This is God's gift to us: "Let this mind be in you, which was also in Christ Jesus" (Phil. 2: 5); "We possess the mind of Christ" (1 Cor. 2: 16); "And be renewed in the spirit of your mind" (Eph. 4: 23).

How does this work out practically? I have found great difficulty here. The Word of God clearly showed me I could have one of two minds. "To set the mind on the flesh is death, but to set the mind on the Spirit is life and peace" (Rom. 8: 6). In my mind I never think of only one thing at a time. We will all quickly agree here! But, joking aside, I think always of two things concurrently, and one of them is always *myself*. Things I hear, read, see, people I meet, etc., I always equate to myself and how it or they affect me. My reaction is always to justify myself, defend myself or congratulate myself according to the nature of the thing I am thinking about. This is the self-mind. This is the flesh-mind of the Scriptures.

Now the opposite is true. All the things I hear, read, see, people I meet, etc., I can equate to Jesus. How does it relate and affect Him? What would He say or do? Any reaction of my will is now of a Christ-mind. This is the mind of the Spirit we read of in the Scriptures.

God can give me the discipline to operate in the

realm of the Christ-mind. All my life, until this crisis, I have thought in the old selfish thought forms. It is very difficult to change overnight. All the most outstanding radical testimonies to which I have listened have shown a period, short or long, for the practice of the new thought forms to oust the old. In the Cross it is immediate by faith. In practice it is a spiritual exercise of discipline. Learn to relate constantly everything of the mind to Christ — not self.

Do not be disheartened by failure. Accept by faith once more the new level of thought life, and think again! The Lord is wonderfully able, merciful and understanding, so entertain no condemnation of the Evil One. "He is a liar, and the father of it" (John 8: 44).

Base Camp then is the place for spiritual re-acclimatisation. First, there must be the admittance and confession of failure. Only then may we receive cleansing from sin. "If we confess our sins, he is faithful and just to forgive us our sins, and to cleanse us from all unrighteousness" (1 John 1: 9). This must be followed by a re-establishing of our devotional life and obedience in our discipleship. "But this one thing I do, forgetting those things which are behind and reaching forth unto those things which are before, I press toward the mark for the prize of the high calling of God in Christ Jesus" (Phil. 3: 13, 14).

Finally, there must be a re-identification with Christ in His death and resurrection. It is here the Blood and the Spirit may cleanse and fill every area of my conscious and sub-conscious life. Then I rise again in a fully baptised life in the Spirit. Thus renewed I look again and move out on to the steeps of the Inner Everest.

8

Assault Plan

ALL THE British assaults on Everest from the year 1921 until 1938 were made from the northern approaches through Tibet. The Ronbuck Glacier led to the North Col, and then to the North Ridge for the highest camps. In 1951 the British attempts made a new reconnaissance through Nepal to the entrance of the Western Cwm on the South Col and summit ridge. The following year the Swiss expedition exploited this new route and in a magnificent endeavour that deserved success placed a Camp Seven on the N.E. ridge at 27,000 ft. above sea level. But Tenzing and Lambert were unable to go much higher. The year 1953 was the year of success. Under Sir John Hunt a camp was established at 27,900 ft. — the ninth of the ascent — from which Tenzing and Sir Edmund Hillary successfully reached the summit at 11.30 a.m. May 29th. Although these series of camps were flexible to meet the conditions of each year and to combat the particular conditions of each assault, they always fell into a general plan of three stages:

Stage 1. Establishment of Advance Base.

Stage 2. Establishment of Assault Camp on South Col.

Stage 3. Assault up the N.E. Ridge.

The question arises, "Is there a similar assault plan for the climb of the Inner Everest?" To me, this calls for serious consideration, for surely, as we have studied the working of His Spirit, whether it be in the reading of the Infallible Word, or listening to the testimonies of the Grace of God in others, or even watching the Spirit teach and deal with fellow-Christians, we see such a variety in number and character of the spiritual experiences of each person. This may have been dictated by the particular personality and character of the person. Some seem to pass through so many experiences of new realisations of God's goodness and love towards them. Each time it brings them into a place of stronger faith and richer fellowship with the Lord. For them there are many camps on the upward ascent. In contrast we may listen to those who speak of but one or two outstanding times of spiritual revelation of God's truth in Christ Jesus, and so have apparently ascended rapidly, with fewer camps, to higher spiritual altitudes.

There is a grave danger today of basic essential truth being made a source of confusion. The use of spiritual terms may have an all-inclusive meaning, or just cover a limited and particular experience. Terminology may be different in meaning according to the doctrine of the church or assembly. The doctrine of the fulness of the Holy Spirit carries quite a varied difference in the thought and opinion of different groups of Christians today. There is a difference of opinion as to how and when He comes into the believer's life. For some it is an all-embracing experience at the crisis of salvation. For others it was a very real experience of grace and faith at a separate time of blessing. Is this experience gained at the first camp on the slopes of our Inner Everest, or at the second camp? Perhaps this experience for some was only reached after several previous camps of blessing! Out of confusion and differences of opinion has arisen antagonism between the Lord's children. Contention stems from the dogmatism with which views are held. Yet again confusion arises through differences in meaning of the terms which are used. In our spiritual discussions, and it is good to speak of the Lord's work in human lives, let us always first define what we mean when using spiritual language. We would then find a great deal of our differences are resolved quickly . . . at least, that is my personal experience. Before we proceed with our ascent, we shall need to find a common ground of agreement of terminology. Can we not therefore find a common scale and measure for our ascent? In the confidence that "We have the mind of Christ" (1 Cor. 2: 16), we should take by faith the unity of minds as revealed in 1 Cor. 1: 10, "That ye all speak the same thing, and that there be no divisions among you, but that ye be perfectly joined together in the same mind and in the same judgment."

Paul told the Ephesians he was praying for them, and that with a special request . . . that the spirit of revelation might be given unto them, that their spiritual blindness through ignorance may be opened to spiritual sight in understanding: he wanted them to realise the riches in Christ, and further, the greatness of His power (Eph. 1: 17–19). This was normal Christian life, but it took many steps of progression to build it up into practical living. He enjoined them to work in peace, purity, power, holiness, truth and light, all these being touched upon in the following chapter (Eph. 2). Our divine Guide prays that we may be given the spiritual revelation to realise and understand the whole of His great plan of Redemption. The answer comes along progressive lessons, stages or camps. As these are attained they unfold

61

the purpose and meaning in the knowledge of the glory of God.

I am personally convinced that no one spiritual experience gives me a "package deal" of blessing. I only obtain from God that which I am consciously in need of, and for which I am desperate in prayer. Am I craving forgiveness? — that is where He meets my need. Am I aware of a powerlessness, or in need of peace, or purity, or rest? It is that very aspect of need that He comes to satisfy and fulfil. The divine economy of spiritual values would be off the gold standard if anything above my realised need were supplied. Yet, even so, *all* is now mine in Christ! God has *now* made all provision, and from His heart of love *all* has been supplied. Hallelujah! But for me is the responsibility to enter in and appropriate the resources for my need.

Thus our camps to the summit may vary. For some there are many camps, for others fewer, yet having said all that, the same trail is to be covered by all of us.

On the real Everest the Assault Plan was in three stages, as already shown, a trinity of advances. Surely we cannot overlook that there is this Divine order of the trinity of values in life. We have the Divine Trinity — God the Father, God the Son and God the Holy Ghost. There is the trinity of man — body, soul and spirit. There is the trinity of evil — the world, the flesh and the devil. Our Lord was Son of God, Son of man, Son of David. On Skull Hill there were three crosses — one on which died a man *in* his sin, on another a man died *to* his sin, and on the third, that central cross, a Man died *for* our sin. The multiplication of these trinities is not the purpose of this chapter, but I recommend for your reading and spiritual profit a booklet by Miss Mary

Bazeley, *The Bible Trinities* (Marshall, Morgan & Scott). Let us apply this law to our assault plan of the Inner Everest. Are there three distinct stages to the highest? Are there three vital steps of obedience that will promote new relationships with God through Jesus Christ? I believe there are such, in our plan of ascent. I submit the three stages:

Stage 1. Salvation

Stage 2. Sanctification

Stage 3. Intercession.

Salvation lifts me up from the Base Camp through and over the Fall. Sanctification takes me to a high point, where I am ready for the summit. Intercession is the summit for the great ministry for which our salvation and sanctification prepared us. It is the life and work of the Holy Spirit within us continuing His ministry for the redemption of souls. But the cost of such a relationship is the extreme limits of human experience. It is the entering into the very sufferings of our Lord for the sake of others which we lack. Paul knew of this when he wrote of himself: "It is now my happiness to suffer for you. This is my way of helping to complete, in my poor human flesh, the full tale of Christ's afflictions still to be endured, for the sake of his body which is the church" (Col. 1: 24).

I use the term Salvation in a more limited sense than is generally understood among evangelicals today. I am personally led to understand that the Lord's teaching on being "born again" is of a greater content than the use and manner of to-day. A lesson I fear we must learn, is that the "only-believe-ism" of so much preaching today is producing a Christian who continues to live in compromise with the world and is subject to backsliding. The "born again" soul *has* new life, new appetites and new associates. The old has passed away and everything has become new. The new life in Christ loves Christ, loves His fellowship and His followers. This new life finds reading the Word of God as essential as the new life of the babe seeks the breast. These are the essential characteristics of being born again of the Spirit of God. May God help us to lift the standard high and make the conditions clear for all to understand.

Then again, the wonderful plan of Salvation is not what God wishes to save me from, but also, and equally so, what He wishes to make me. "Follow Me, and I will *make* you . . ." is the emphasis of His teaching. This is what He desires us to be *in* Christ, as well as what He is doing for us through Christ. But it is more than this, for we need the eyes of our understanding opened much more widely to the former, the subjective emphasis in Christ. We need the metamorphosis of experience to make the Word become flesh in us (John 1: 14). I understand Salvation to be the simple initial act of faith in Christ. "Believe on the Lord Jesus Christ, and thou shalt be saved, and thy house" (Acts 16: 31), or "For the word of the cross is folly to those who are perishing, but to us who are being saved it is the power of God" (1 Cor. 1: 18). To be saved can be but the first step of a "so great salvation" which embraces the highest relationship in Christ. But, as I have mentioned, I accept Salvation to cover confession, separation and restitution, the manward responsibility. His suffering, substitution and sacrifice on the Cross is God's heart of love forgiving me and bringing me into a new relationship with Himself.

Sanctification is God dealing with me. He calls

64

for my consecration and crucifixion. My obedience leads to the abundant full and overflowing filling of His Spirit in sanctifying power.

Intercession is God working His purposes of the redemption of others *through* me. He begins by bringing me to a place of Vision. I see what God is after through me. Then I am led down into Identification with that purpose — a costly walk in every sense of life. Then and then only is the Great Intercessor able to intercede through me. I become a channel of His interceding ministry for others. This is the summit.

PART TWO

THE ASCENT

9

Camp One — Confession

WE NOW leave Base Camp for the camp by camp ascent to the summit. This first stage takes me through the Ice-Fall. The three camps necessary to do this have a particular significance when applied to this part of the spiritual progress called Salvation.

The Inner Everest is a personal challenge. Therefore the emphasis will obviously be upon personal responsibility and the cost. This will not in any possible way mean that one is not aware of the Godward aspect of Salvation and the wonder of Divine Grace. The emphasis is purposely made on the manward responsibilities, as I feel this is the lack and unemphasised aspect of spiritual truth.

Dore, in his illustration of Dante, has a striking picture representing Dante and his companions approaching the gates of Repentance. Leading up to the gates are three steps. These are the three elements which are necessary for true repentance. The first step is Contrition, the second is Confession and the third is Restitution:

"Thither did we draw nigh, and that first stair
Was of white marble, polished so and clear;
It mirrored all my features as they were.
The second, darker than dusk was seen
Of stone all rugged, rough and coarse in grain
With many a crack its length and breadth between.
The third which over all others tower amain,

Appeared as if of fiery porphyry,
Like blood that gushes crimson from the vein."

Thus the first camp is a revelation to the climber of
his actual condition. The second calls for a disassocia-
tion from the old life. The third is only reached in
restitution and reparation. But the spiritual climber
already now begins to sense the new world ahead —
a world in which his soul is cleansed through the
blood of Christ. Forgiveness has brought him to a
new relationship. Emerging from the seracs —
jumbled mass of towering ice blocks on a glacier —
of sin he sees the open ground rising steeply away.
It's grand to be alive with abundant life. Opening the
Guide Book we are given a closer detailed account of
this part of the ascent.

The Holy Spirit clothes the basic premises in the
story of a son coming back from a far country to his
father, who for a long time has patiently watched the
road for this moment of return. Read all about it
in Luke 15.

As soon as the lad is in earshot of his father he
cries, "Dad, I have sinned — against God, against
you." The lad knew what the obstacle was to his
reception at home. He confesses. This is God's
prior condition to forgiveness: "Repentance for the
forgiveness of sins" (Luke 3: 3). "If we confess our
sins, he is faithful and just to forgive us our sins"
(1 John 1: 9). The word "confess" is the Greek word
"homologeo" meaning "to speak the same thing"
concerning our sin. I have got to agree with God
and speak in the same terms of the sin which is the
obstacle to reconciliation in forgiveness.

God invites us to reason with Him on the issue.
"Come now, let us argue it out, says the Lord.
Though your sins are scarlet, they may become white

as snow" (Isa. 1: 18). But why argue? So that He can bring us to see sin from His viewpoint. I have no difficulty then in saying also what God says about my sin.

There was a crisis in the camp of Israel. They had been defeated in battle. The reason was a sin of disobedience by Achan. Joshua confronted the culprit: "My son, give honour to the Lord the God of Israel and make your confession to him" (Josh. 7: 19). Here "confession" is the Hebrew word "todah", meaning to "cast up the hand", a sign even today of admittance, agreement and acknowledgement.

We have to admit that it is the most difficult thing in the world for a man to see the sinfulness of his sin. It blinds his moral and spiritual eyesight. The Sacred Record states concerning Judas leaving to betray Jesus, "He immediately went out; and it was night" (John 13: 30). It was night — in more than one sense. Whenever a man goes out to sin, he goes out into darkness. "He who hates his brother is in *the* darkness" (1 John 2: 11).

H. G. Wells, the British novelist and a writer not disposed to Christian ways of thought, writes a parable of a legendary land where all the inhabitants are blind. The only man who can see is a visitor to this land. Because of his very ability to see he is persecuted and despised. The inhabitants of this country could not see, and from the centuries of blindness came the belief that there was no such thing as sight!

The true "country of the blind" is this old world of ours in which we live. There came One with full and perfect vision — we put Him to death on the Cross.

The reason for our blindness is our sin. The quarrelsome man thinks everyone unreasonable —

except himself. The revengeful man thinks he is animated by a proper self-respect. The discontented man scarcely thinks the trouble is where it really lies. James Martineau, a British Unitarian theologian and philosopher, no matter how we may disagree with his position, makes this dynamic remark in his sermon *Christ's treatment of Guilt*, "Moral evil is the *only* thing in creation of which it is decreed that the more we are familiar with it, the less we know of it."

Emperor Theodosius, in A.D. 390, entered Milan after the massacre of 1,500 citizens of Thessalonica. The Emperor proceeded to the cathedral after being excommunicated by the church through reason of his crime. He was stopped at the cathedral door by the intrepid Bishop Ambrose who forbade him entrance until he had made public confession of his crime. The Emperor pleaded that if he were guilty of homicide, so was King David, a man after God's own heart. Ambrose sternly replied, "You have imitated David in his crime, now imitate him in his repentance." He drove him from the cathedral precincts.

Newman, a British theologian and author of the well-known hymn *Lead, kindly Light*, said, "We have lost our best defence against sin when we cease to be shocked by it." Now we can understand why the Lord emphasised this darkness with the words, "how great is that darkness" (Matt. 6: 23).

The more we see of the blinding effect of sin on the mind and conscience, the more deeply we realise how impossible it is for us to acknowledge our sin and to "speak the same thing" regarding it as God speaks. As impossible almost as a blind man in a dark room chasing a black cat that is not there!

How then do we meet this problem? This is the power of Rom. 10: 14, "But how are men to call (epikaleo=to call in one to help) upon him in whom they have not believed?" The question is answered, "So faith comes from what is heard, and what is heard comes by the preaching of Christ" (Rom. 10: 17).

God's divine ministry by His Spirit through His Word, His ambassadors, and His creation brings the light to reveal, to help me to see the obstacle to my return to God in Christ. Now I can see, and seeing I cast up my hands in agreement with what God has said about my condition. I confess. Camp One is reached.

10

Camp Two — Separation

BEFORE starting this chapter I turned the pages of the official account of the assault of Everest by Sir John Hunt, and at the same time read snatches of Sir Edmund Hillary's own personal account of the attack on this most vicious and dangerous section of Everest — the Ice-Fall.

The diagram in the official account shows that nearly half the camps established were taken in ascending the Ice-Fall. This shows only too dramatically what this section calls for in terms of energy, objectives and manpower. Let me quote Sir Edmund Hillary's impressions of these particular days of climbing: "The route ahead did not look much better. It was just a jumble of ice blocks. I started ferreting a way through them. Sometimes I could squeeze between two of the blocks, sometimes I had to cut a trail over the top and on mercifully few occasions I had to make a route almost down underneath them. It was nerve-racking work and progress was inevitably very slow . . . Discouraged, tired, and not a little scared we decided to call it a day, and slowly made our way back to the comforts and safety of Base Camp." A sketch map of the Ice-Fall on page 140 of *High Adventure* by Sir Edmund shows names of the various parts of the climb up the Ice-Fall. These names speak for themselves: "Hillary's Horror", "Hell-fire Alley", "Mike's Horror", "Atom Bomb Area" and "Nutcracker". Your mind can picture the experiences that prompted these names.

I have taken pains to share the above, as the spiritual counterpart is a close, very close parallel. The demands upon me are very real. The devil's assault to wipe out any spiritual progress is fierce, frightening and often wearing upon the young Christian. For this reason the camps of "spiritual decision" are fast close one upon another. Not too distant above Camp Confession is the hell-fire-alley to Camp Separation. On the ascent of the Inner Everest this section has eliminated many a climber. They have ever remained among the depressing debris of the Fall — unhappy, depressed and defeated. This hell-fire-alley to Separation must be climbed. It is the way up and out to wide horizons and purer heights. The Scriptures tell us that the challenge of Separation has created casualties in the dawn-days of discipleship. Listen! Jesus is speaking to a young man who had much of this world's goods — "If you wish to go the whole way, go, sell your possessions, and give to the poor, and then you will have riches in heaven; and come, follow me. When the young man heard this, he went away with a heavy heart; for he was a man of great wealth" (Matt. 19: 21, 22). The circumstances here are immaterial to the highlighting of the superlative premise that he who loves himself above all else turns his back on the Lord Jesus Christ. To love oneself is to love one's right to decide where I shall go, what I shall do, and whom I shall choose to accompany me. Self is always, inevitably a precursor to sin. "There is a way which seems right to a man, but its end is the way to death" (Prov. 14: 12).

This man-way is the broad way. It has got to be left as soon as possible to find the God-way, the narrow way.

A teacher asked her class of boys to define the

word "repentance". One hand shot up with the explosive reply, "To be sorry enough to quit." He was bang-on.

The Lost Son was in no two minds as to the next step (Luke 15: 18). He knew there could be no further remaining in the land of women and wine, wantonness and wickedness. The son had to get back to the father for the forgiveness to be absolute.

The Rev. A. W. Tozer of North America declares that there has appeared in modern times a new evangelical message. This new appeal, he comments, brings me another cross. It is light and smooth, easy to carry. It does not chafe and hurt like the old rugged Cross. Again, it seeks to *re-direct* my life into a new association with this world. The old Cross slew my sin. The new cross helps me to re-accommodate myself to the world. This new cross carries a message that if the Father of the Lost Son knew where he was the Father would say, "I will arise and go unto my son, I will save him the long journey back and the embarrassment of his admitting a failure. I will help him in his misfortune" (not his sin, please note). Such a parable and such a cross is *never* found between the covers of God's infallible Book. For Bible students it is interesting to note there are forty-seven uses of four Hebrew words associated with the Christian's injunction to separate from sin. There are ten uses of five Greek words which are emphatic, dogmatic and without ambiguity telling me that I must neither touch nor hold on to sin and its derivatives. I am to withdraw from, put aside, place at a distance anything pertaining to sin.

The caretaker (janitor) of a church I was visiting some years ago kept switching the lights on and off! The congregation had stayed around long after the meeting talking with friends and renewing long-term acquaintances. I'm afraid they had forgotten the caretaker who had to clear and tidy up before locking the doors to go home. We were unconsciously inconsiderate.

Only one light was on when a man came from the shadows and stood in front of me. "Please help me," he pleaded. The caretaker was now in a back room working, so I snatched a few moments. "Tell me your problem as simply and quickly as possible." I heard a brief, shattering confession to a shackling habit of homosexuality that was driving the poor fellow to extreme desperation. The time and personal counsel this situation required was just not possible, and the caretaker was now coming towards me. I took out a piece of paper and wrote down the name and address of a pastor, a dear friend of mine in a nearby city. "Go and see him. Tell him you come from me." Shaking hands we parted. A couple of weeks later came the thrilling news of this man's complete and utter deliverance, a miracle of God's grace and power. A year passed before I met my pastor friend and learned of the tragic downfall of this man and the recurrence of this devilish practice. It happened one night when he had little to do and was feeling at a loose end. He decided to stroll around an area of the town which was one of the old haunts of his previous associates. That's all there was to it. He walked straight into it! That dear man ought to have kept out of that area. One cannot touch again the things from which we have been delivered and remain unburnt. The Bible command is clear and concise, "And therefore, come away and leave them, separate yourselves, says the Lord; touch nothing unclean. Then I will accept you, says the Lord" (2 Cor. 6: 17, 18).

In finalising this chapter let us make the test as to

whether we have reached Camp Two (Separation). Kneel with me in prayer. We are going to ask the Holy Spirit to be a witness and judge through our minds on the issues which follow. "Lord, by Thy Holy Spirit, judge my life now regarding its separation unto You. I am willing, Lord, to be obedient. Please speak to me on this issue that I may be as You want me to be unto Yourself. Amen."

Let us look first of all at our hands. Is that a ring on your left hand third finger? Engaged? Is he or she a committed Christian as you desire to be? If so, God bless you both. If not, the Spirit says, "Do not unite yourselves with unbelievers; they are no fit mates for you. What has righteousness to do with wickedness?" (2 Cor. 6: 14). The Lord will give grace and strength to take the decisive step that must be taken.

Is that your bookshelf over there? Can we have a look? Would you feel embarrassed if He pulled that and that one out? That magazine is not far off pornography, is it? Clean it up, dear friend, clean up the bookshelves.

I see you are a music lover and have a good collection of records — what is your line? Classic, pop, rock and roll, 'blue'? Could you sit with Jesus and enjoy that record that finds its origin in "schitz" and "spiritism"? Throw it out. The test is to be able to put that record on for Jesus. There are records of humour, life-expression, and works of the masters He would enjoy. The Holy Spirit will be infallible in His decision. Of course, there are the border-line decisions. The answer here is revealed in a boy's request to his mother. Standing at the top of the stairs he yells, "Mum! Is this blue shirt of mine clean?" Mother calls back, "I do not know — but if it is doubtful — it is dirty!"

You have now reached Camp Two.

11

Camp Three — Restitution

CAMP THREE will bring us to the top of the "Fall" where our fellowship with God will be fully restored. God established that fellowship with us by His suffering, substitution and sacrifice. These three great doctrinal statements clothe deep experiences that anyone who forgives must accept. God can forgive as He fully embraced all the suffering I caused Him. He stood in my place and accepted the condemnation I should have received. He felt the punishment that should have been laid on me. Thereby He is empowered to forgive and to save. Now He awaits the three steps I must take in confessing my sin and need, in separating myself to follow Him, leaving all others. And any forgiveness that at all plumbs depths of love to renew again a fellowship valued and lost, will *want* to make restitution or reparation. It is inherent in our psychological approach. It is revealed every time full forgiveness is enjoyed. I see it enacted in small ways almost daily.

The climb to Camp Three is short, sharp and difficult.

Let us go back to the Lost Son in Luke 15: 19–21. Throwing himself into his father's arms, he sobs, "I am no longer worthy to be called your son; treat me as one of your hired servants." The word "worthy" is the Greek "axios" meaning "worth in return". It gives the idea of not being able to make the restitution of returning as a son, but feeling he can give only the value of a hired servant.

This requirement of restitution is supported by the three Persons of the Trinity.

God declares, in the record of the foundation laws as found in Exodus 21 and 22, that restitution is a basic requirement of the evidences towards the desire and experience of forgiveness. Repentance, without a desire to seek to make good the consequences of sin, is no true repentance at all.

Jesus shows how restitution is acceptable when He listens to the declaration of Zaccheus to give fourfold in return wherever he had extracted in excess from the taxpayers. Jesus commends him and states that salvation has come to his house. He was a true spiritual son of Abraham. Salvation was granted as the three signs of repentance were evident. "Behold, Lord, the half of my goods I give to the poor" reveals a new disposition separating him from the old manner of life: "And if I have taken any thing from any man by false accusation" concedes his confession: "I will restore him fourfold" is tantamount to his act of restitution (Luke 19: 8).

The Holy Spirit has always led to the restitution and restoration of goods by those who have come under a *deep* sense of need for gracious pardon.

There was a great move of the Spirit of God in Finland in 1939. The Government Treasury of the country received a tremendous windfall that year. "A most remarkable circumstance," said Aane Linturi, chief of the Revenue Department. In each case the evaders of income tax had volunteered their names and addresses and had stated they had come under conviction through the clear speaking of God to them in a period of revival.

A youth was under deep consciousness of sin and was crying out for forgiveness. He was suddenly conscious of God putting His finger on a fact in his life. Obediently he returned his degree to the Vice-Chancellor of his old University. He knew he had used illegal help when sitting his finals.

A Christian minister, after twenty years of barrenness and burden, sent back £35 that had been wrongfully acquired.

Refused restitution blocked blessing. Obedience released the grace of God to very many souls.

George Müller, in his youth, stole from others. But he also found the avenue to spiritual power was bordered with confession and restitution.

I was twenty-one years of age and had completed my apprenticeship at the British Thompson Houston Co. in Harlesden, North London. God led me into training for the foreign mission field. Very early in this period of preparation God began to deal with me. One issue was a source of horror and fear. God wanted me to make restitution to my old firm. I had on many occasions gone to the waste boxes to sort out metal for various "do-it-yourself" jobs at home. A radio project, a cycle repair, etc. had needed copper, brass, nuts and bolts. I found all I required in the scrap bins at work. God put His finger on this for restitution. I knew, too, how much I ought to pay! But what would the outcome be of being a self-confessed thief? I imagined a policeman at the college door, arrest and terrible sentences! I dare not do it. It would ruin my Christian character and missionary hopes. But God was relentless. The journey to Camp Three was the shortest in distance, the longest in time, and the most fearful part of the ascent I have known.

The letter dropped into the letter box and £x was

on its way to the British Thompson Houston Co., London. I heard the letter drop. It was irretrievable. The die was cast. Instead of tautening tension I felt a pervading peace. I confess a measure of anxiety and apprehension remained. One morning a British Thompson Houston headed envelope was put in my letter rack. Now for it! It had not been a policeman at any rate. I read, "Dear Mr. Moules, Your letter and remittance have been received. On behalf of the British Thompson Houston Co. I would like to express deep appreciation for the letter stating what prompted your action, and we wish you every success in your new life, and future.

Yours sincerely."

I was perplexed! I was wished success instead of prison sentence! I was *so* happy. I laughed and praised God in one breath. But, deep down under this emotional reaction, I was conscious of a spiritual touch from God.

So often restitution seems beyond our power, even to fellow men. But it is God against whom I have sinned. How can I make reparation to a holy, almighty God? We can bring a willingness and readiness of heart. "Thou desirest truth in the inward being" (Psa. 51: 6). This truth is a fidelity. God may ask of us a token reparation to test this readiness. Only the Spirit has the right to show how and where restitution may be made. Only the Spirit of God can give the enabling to do it.

Above the Fall I know now a full and free salvation. Charles Wesley knew this experience of free pardoning grace when he sang, "My chains fell off, my heart was free; I rose, went forth, and followed Thee."

It is Jesus only meeting our every need. It is He

who makes pardon free, gracious and unmerited. In rejoicing in this precious experience let us begin to understand the cost and condition the Father met to make our reconciliation.

A story is told of a soldier who died fighting for his country. The news came to the mother through a War Office communique. She was inconsolable. "If I might only see him for five minutes," she prayed. An angel came to her to say her prayer had been heard and she could choose five minutes only of the thirty years of his life. "How would you see him?" the angel asked. She pondered. Should she see him as he nobly died at his post; or should it be as he, flushed and joyous, received his school honour; or just five minutes of babyhood? No, none of these she decided. "I would have him as he ran in from the garden to ask forgiveness for being naughty. He was so small and so unhappy. He was hot with the tears streaking white down his grubby face. He flew to my arms with such force — he hurt me!"

Do you get the message?

12

Camp Four — Consecration

TWO MILES of an ice-valley lay before them. When the great climber Leigh Mallory saw it during the first reconnaissance of Everest in 1921, he named it the Western Cwm, doubtless from his affection for the mountains of Wales where climbing haunts were to be found. At the head of this great valley lies the trinity of peaks, Everest 29,002 ft., Lhotse 27,890 ft., and Nuptse 25,680 ft. Thus contained between Everest and Nuptse, this astonishing freak of nature leads the climber to the very foot of the Everest pyramid. It is the focal point of ascent. The assault up the valley marks the distinct second stage of the three-stage ascent. Camps Four, Five and Six were established along the floor of the ice-valley to the "overhang" of Everest.

Our ascent of the Inner Everest also finds us now at the beginning of a new aspect of our life with Christ. The ascent of the Fall has brought us into renewed fellowship with God Himself. Now, God, in Christ, by His Spirit, begins to work on the life that has just been redeemed by His grace and love. The disciples heard the words, "Follow me, and I will make you fishers of men" (Matt. 4: 19). To be called to follow Christ is a high honour, higher indeed than any honour men can bestow upon each other. Jesus Christ is a Man come to save men. In Him the divine nature is married to our human nature, and wherever human nature exists there is the raw material from which He makes followers and saints.

Our Lord recognises no distinction of class or social status, male or female. His invitation is to all. He calls us that He may make us. He makes us that He may use us.

There is only one place in the Scriptures where I find direct speech of the Lord describing the Church, which is His Bride, of which you and I are individual members. The characteristics of the individual are the characteristics of the Church. Let us frankly examine ourselves against the divine standard. The blue-print is found in the Song of Solomon. In its original intent it was to show the relationship between God and His people, the Jews. Today it comes to us as a picture of the Lord's relationship with His Church; with you and me. The Lord is speaking, locking up the wonderful meaning in Eastern idiom and expression. "A garden locked is my sister, my bride, a garden locked, a fountain sealed. Your shoots are an orchard of pomegranates with all choicest fruits, henna with nard, nard and saffron, calamus and cinnamon, with all trees of frankincense, myrrh and aloes, with all chief spices — a garden fountain, a well of living water, and flowing streams from Lebanon. Awake, O north wind, and come, O south wind! Blow upon my garden, let its fragrance be wafted abroad. Let my beloved come to his garden, and eat its choicest fruits" (Song 4: 12–16).

Let us take the statements one at a time.

"A garden locked is my sister, my bride." An alternative translation is a walled garden and locked. During the last war I spent some months in Palestine and travelled throughout the Holy Land. One day I strolled over Galilean hills. The season was dry and very hot. The grass of the hillside was brown and dry. Below me lay a little village of white-washed houses, made picturesque by the trees and the well nearby. The hillside was dry and void of colour except for an oblong of the richest green to be seen. What a contrast! My eyes went back to it again and again. I dropped downhill for a closer look and the answer was obvious — it was a garden. The walls were high at 8–10 ft. to keep out the ubiquitous goat and gazelle. If these animals had got in every vestige of green would have disappeared overnight! The walls of the garden spoke of separation, emphasised in our last chapter.

I found the door and gained entrance. Those high walls around breathed of security and safety within. Here lies the great spiritual law that the safety of my spiritual life from backsliding is equated to my separation from the world. Jesus says His bride is separated unto Him. So often people speak of having to give up things and separate from the old associates in following Christ. Why, oh why, speak so negatively of this terrific fellowship I have gained with Christ? I am not separated *from* anything, but separated *unto* Christ. The former pales into insignificance against the latter.

"A fountain sealed." In the centre of the garden I saw a spring. It was sealed by an arrangement of stones around the site, and a flat stone acting as a cover. The water bubbled out between the stones, yet the source was kept clean from leaves, dirt and fouling by plough animals that came in from time to time.

Where did this water come from? If you looked over the wall you would see, in the high heat haze, the ghostly shape of snowy Mt. Hermon. The heavy dews of Hermon together with the melting snows form subterranean streams which irrigate the world famous olive groves on the lower slopes. Other streams break the surface further afield. Around each a garden is developed. Hermon spoke to the Jewish people of God's overshadowing Presence. Thus these streams are symbolic of the Holy Spirit coming from God Himself to the separated life of every believer. "Sealed", that the water may be unsullied, must obviously speak of an ungrieved Holy Spirit in my life as I walk in continual obedience.

"Your shoots are an orchard of pomegranates." The pomegranate fruit, red amongst the deep green leaves, was the superlative expression of beauty. In England, we would speak of an English rose garden! Jesus says His Church is beautiful to look upon. Your life and mine catches the eye because of its purity and love. Well may I hang my head in shame and ask myself if it really does attract to the Lord Jesus.

Now comes the list of the contents of the garden. May I point out that not one tree is native to Palestine. All have been imported. If there is one lesson I want the reader to clearly understand and learn, it is that only what God sanctifies and puts in my life that is acceptable to Him. Often I have heard young people testify that they are going to use *their* voices for Jesus, or *their* musical talents, *their* varied and many qualifications to be used for Jesus. There is a mistaken understanding that all I have to do for consecration is to use the old skills and talents now for Jesus! Nothing can be further from the truth.

Moses came to God concerning the deliverance of the children of Israel. He had a shepherd staff in his hand — symbolic of his secular life and calling. God said, "What is that in your hand?" Moses replied, "A rod." God enjoined him to lay it down. Immediately it underwent a metamorphosis and God told Moses to take it by the tail. He obeyed and the staff (rod) again took shape in his hand. God then commissioned Moses, "That they may believe that the Lord, the God of their fathers, the God of Abraham, the God of Isaac, and the God of Jacob, has appeared to you" (Exod. 4: 2–5).

In consecration I lay *all* at His feet. I am empty-handed. It is *not* a change of use of my old "flairs" and "abilities". I await what God gives back to me, sanctified for His use. He may not give me back any of the old qualifications to use for Him. God may grant new gifts entirely. In our Art Studio at W.E.C. Headquarters is one who is spiritually gifted in art projects for books and magazines — but she was a nurse to begin with. The founder of Radio Worldwide was a company director and accountant. Today God has developed in him His gift for radio programming that has strikingly changed an old format for a new, making "ears to hear" worldwide. Only what God plants grows to yield acceptable fruit.

Finally, let us look at the trees and plants of the garden. They represent the ministries of the Body of Christ — His Church. Note as you read with what each is associated, and how the basic ingredient is obtained.

Camphire (Henna) — comes from the Middle East. Its use is for perfume and fragrance. It is released by the agitation of the bush by hand or the wind.

Spikenard — Himalayas; used in ointment for healing. Obtained by crushing the "spike" of the plant.

Saffron — Europe; used both medically and for dyeing. It is a healing agent. Obtained by powdering the leaves.

Calamus — India; used in the anointing oil for services and also in sweet incense. Speaks of prayer. Obtained by bruising the joints of the bamboo-like cane.

Cinnamon — Ceylon; used in the anointing oil for service. Obtained by burning the bark.

Frankincense — Arabia; used in the anointing oil and sweet incense, speaking of intercession. Obtained by incising the bark and "bleeding" the gum from the tree.

Myrrh — Arabia and Africa; used in the anointing oil. Speaks of sacrifice. Obtained by burying and rotting the tree for months and then pressing out the oil.

Aloes — S.E. Asia; ointment for perfume. Used in an asepsis application. Speaks of incorruption. Obtained by drying and pulverising the plant.

Spices (Aromatic) — from many countries; used in sweet incense and speaks of the graces of Christ. Obtained in many ways such as by drying and powdering the plant.

This is the complete picture as Christ sees His Church. He sees me separated to Himself and living a life of obedience pleasing to the Holy Spirit. My life is attractive with a fragrant influence. The Lord Himself has placed in me the ministry or gift He desires of me. It may be a healing touch on broken lives as well as upon stricken physical bodies. He may ask of me a life of prayer or of more costly intercession. It could be that the anointing oil will send me for service far afield or at home.

13

Camp Five — Crucifixion

SHADOWS may sometimes give us an idea,
though somewhat distorted, of what the real
object is like. Human analogies always break down
when used to illustrate spiritual truth. But I do
want this essential truth to come through to you, and
will sketch a shadow to contribute to the real
dimension of this spiritual truth.

Four men were huddled together high up on a
Himalayan giant. They were the assault party and
second assault and supporting pair. The intense
cold and wicked wind had played havoc with the
resources of all the men. But one of the climbers
was in no fit condition to go on, nor was he fit to
be permitted to struggle out of that little tent into the
furious elements outside to battle his way down to a
lower camp. Someone would have to go down with
him. It was not merely going down that called for
a decision. But one of these three remaining men,
each of whom wanted above all else to stand on the
summit the next day, would have to make a decision
that eliminated him from that attack and success.
There was a significant pause and silence, broken
only by the gun-crack of the whipping canvas of the
tent under the blast of the gale. One of the climbers
struggled to release himself from the sleeping bag.
"I'll go down — every success to you both." Roped
together two men felt their way down to safety. One
of them knew what it was to "die" to high personal
ambition for the sake of another; for the sake of the

expedition's success. This is only the shadow.

Paul the Apostle spells it out in another dimension. "I have been crucified with Christ: the life I now live is not my life, but the life which Christ lives in me: and my present bodily life is lived by faith in the Son of God" (Gal. 2: 20). This means that the bodily activity goes on unchanged, but my mind, will and emotions that operate in this body are taken over by the Lord Jesus Christ Himself. It is no longer I — but Christ.

The old idea that I serve Jesus to the best of my ability is good — but it is the enemy of the best, the highest, which is Jesus working through me. I am only a channel, an instrument, for the flow of the executive of the Godhead, which is the Spirit. I am not the executive.

If Jesus is to come through, then I am to get out of the way — in fact so completely removed that it is a death experience. No other symbol would be sufficiently adequate to illustrate this truth. The Cross always every time.

But the Rev. A. W. Tozer puts it another way, "There is something less among us. We would do well to identify it so that we may repudiate it. That something is a poetic fiction, a product of the romantic imagination and maudlin religious fancy. It is a Jesus, gentle, dreamy, shy and sweet and almost effeminate. He is marvellously adaptable to any society He may find Himself in. He is cooed over by women disappointed in love, patronised by pro tem. celebrities, recommended by psychiatrists as a model of a well-integrated personality. He is used as a means to any carnal end, but He is never acknowledged as Lord. These quasi-Christians follow a quasi-Christ. They want His help — not His interference. They will flatter Him but never obey Him.   Salvation does not come by mere 'accepting the finished work' or 'deciding for Christ'. It comes by believing on the Lord Jesus Christ, the whole, living victorious Lord who, as God and man fought our fight and won it, accepted our debt as His own and paid it, took our sins and died under them and rose again to set us free.   This is the true Christ, and nothing less will do."   The decision for a crucifixion experience is mine and none other.

We should take up again the description of the Church as we found it in the Song of Solomon. Here the Lord has finished speaking, and the Bride replies.   The Church, you and I, must re-echo this command.   "Awake, O north wind, and come, O south wind!   Blow upon my garden, let its fragrance be wafted abroad.   Let my beloved come to his garden, and eat its choicest fruits" (Song 4: 16).

These winds are destructive.   While I was in Iran during the last war, a cold north wind blew which immobilised a whole armoured battalion and made roads impassable with broken boughs and fallen trees.   On another occasion, during the hot season, I left Gaza in a military convoy about 8 a.m.   At 10 a.m. we stopped for a short rest.   I was dressed in tropical kit and in unscrewing my thermos flask allowed my arm to rest on the metal mudguard — I was skinned from elbow to wrist!   The hot south wind, Khamseen, had been blowing on the convoy since we left Gaza.   Our metal vehicles were blistering hot.

Imagine these winds on a garden.   The breaking and destruction of the north wind.   The blistering, drying, withering that would result from the south wind.   No longer an ordered garden — but one pitiful to look upon.   But surely these were the very processes that released the basic ingredients of the

90

trees. Incising, burning, burying and powdering were necessary for the balsams to flow. That is why the Bride ventures on in her invitation, this time to the Lord Himself, "Let my beloved come to his garden, and eat its choicest fruits."

Only the Cross can release the choicest gifts in my life, and I must invite its impression upon me. The Lord will not force me to carry this Cross. I must go willingly and in His love embrace it.

My brother Percy, ten years older than I, was a missionary in the Congo. With his able wife Edith, they opened a leprosarium, treating almost a thousand leprosy patients. The work was demanding until they were exhausted and were in real need of a rest. Leaving Nebobongo they planned a period of rest and recuperation in Ruanda. On the way my brother contracted typhoid. With no resources to fight the disease he was, within hours, fighting feebly for his life. Edith shared with me how she flung herself by the bed and pleaded for Percy's life.

But there was another issue in their lives. The medical side of the work had been most successful and had received a Belgian honour. But the spiritual response had been so little. They had prayed that they were willing for any price to see blessing fall on the lives of those at "Nebo". While Edith was agonising on her knees for Percy's life, God asked her a question, so gently, "What do you want — Percy's life or blessing at Nebobongo? 'Except a corn of wheat fall into the ground and die, it abideth alone: but if it die, it bringeth forth much fruit' (John 12: 24)." Edith sobbed, "Not my will, Lord; You choose." Percy died. Nebobongo felt the wind of God's blessing blow upon those many sufferers.

Several years later Edith was dying of cancer in London. One desire remained, to see the leprosy work commenced in Portuguese Guinea. This would also confirm the Mission's continued work in that land. The Governor of Portuguese Guinea had graciously received her and had promised to support her application to his Government. But for a long time there had been no news.

Edith was excited when she learned that the Governor had arrived in Lisbon. She would go to him. For a dying woman whose bone structure was honeycombed by the disease this was no journey to be taken at all. But she knew it was God's will, cost what it may. By invalid chair and stretcher she was carried to the plane and then to Lisbon and was settled comfortably in a hotel. She wrote asking for an audience with the Governor. His response was to hurry to her hotel where he reaffirmed his intention and promised to expedite the matter. Edith flew home to London and was soon in the presence of the Lord, but not before she knew that the message of the Gospel that deals with man, body, soul and spirit was assured as a continued ministry in Portuguese Guinea.

"It is no longer I who live, but Christ who lives in me" (Gal. 2: 20).

14

Camp Six — Sanctification

SANCTIFICATION is the last camp of the second stage of God's preparation of His follower, and a very important place at which to arrive. This is the relationship where God alone can act. Sanctification is God's sovereign work. Consecration and crucifixion are my preparation, by His grace and strength, for this divine prerogative. I cannot sanctify myself. "Sanctify them through thy truth: thy word is truth" (John 17: 17), are the words of the Lord Jesus Christ when praying for the disciples. Paul, speaking of Christ's relationship with His Church, says, "That he might sanctify her, having cleansed her by the washing of water with the word" (Eph. 5: 26); "The very God of peace sanctify you wholly" (1 Thess. 5: 23); "That he might sanctify the people with his own blood" (Heb. 13: 12).

When God sanctifies a man or woman three things happen. First, God will fill you with His Holy Spirit. "If the Spirit of him who raised Jesus from the dead dwells within you, then the God who raised Christ Jesus from the dead will also give new life to your mortal bodies through his indwelling Spirit" (Rom. 8: 11). "That ye might be filled with all the fulness of God" (Eph. 3: 19).

To be filled means just that; every aspect of my life — conscious and subconscious mind, will, emotions, life physical and life spiritual — comes under the influence and control of the Holy Spirit. This precious experience has come in different ways to us all. For some it has been an outstanding crisis when God floods the soul with love and joy until emotion can contain it no longer. Others have no dramatic testimony to share. For them the deep sense of peace rested over their whole personality. However He comes by His Spirit, be it by the simile of an earthquake, wind and fire, or by a still small Voice of assurance — we know the Lord has come.

Very often systemised doctrines err by stating the particular way and manner the Spirit may come. Scripture and spiritual experience declare Him to come as He will and when He will. God will not sanctify to my terms of reference.

Life is flowing at full flood when the blessing comes to the believer. Never before has everything been so relevant, worth while and satisfying. Joy and happiness are deepened to indescribable dimensions. Life is life abundant. True manhood and womanhood is in the spiritual maturing by God's Holy Spirit.

The second aspect of God's work of Grace is that He gives to His sanctified child a spiritual gift or gifts. The great failing of the Church today is a failure to expect, recognise or use the gifts of the Spirit. They are essential for the work lying ahead. The Church of Christ, or the fellowship of believers, needs to be protected from evil onslaughts that intend to disintegrate the body of Christ and nullify the work of the Spirit. The Church needs teaching, revelation, administration, authority and power as its credentials. The Church is geared to evangelism and healing. Each emphasis has its spiritual gift for the enabling.

Particularly these days should we take careful note of the Spirit's working, both in individuals and in the wider outpourings in the world today. Since 1965

there has been a new dimension of the Spirit's manifestation in the world. It is a work of God. Because
the Spirit broke all bounds of narrow terms of
reference, the conservative evangelicals were thrown
immediately on the defensive. It would have been
good for them to have marked the words of Gamaliel
in Acts 5: 38. "For if this teaching or movement is
merely human it will collapse of its own accord. But
if it should be from God you cannot defeat them, and
you might actually find yourselves to be fighting
against God!" From mature and revered men of
God has come the condemnation that it is of the
devil. How near can we come to blasphemy! Over
the last two years we have seen a far greater accep-
tance of the Spirit's work in the world. The devil
has made sure that he has marketed a counterfeit.
Again, the Church itself has marred its testimony by
its excesses. It has gone from the Spiritual to
fleshy exhibitionism. Error finds easy victims when
it makes an experience the "be-all and end-all" of
spiritual life and worship. Christ, and only Christ,
is the centre of my life and love. Anything else is
idolatry — even spiritual experience! Never seek
experience — only Him.

Before leaving this aspect, a word should be said
about the teaching of many in Pentecostal move-
ments and charismatic fellowships that speaking in
an unknown tongue is the only authentic evidence
that the Spirit's baptism has been received.

This is built upon the experience of some who are
recorded in the Acts of the Apostles as having been
filled with the Spirit accompanied by this manifestation. We are directed to the day of Pentecost (Acts
2: 1-4), to the household of Cornelius at Caesarea,
(Acts 10:44-48), and to the twelve disciples at Ephesus,
(Acts 19: 1-7). But we are not told why there is no

reference to tongues in the case of the new converts in Samaria being filled with the Spirit, Acts 8: 17, or in the case of the Apostle Paul, Acts 9: 17–19. Three cases out of five is hardly a basis for such a divisive doctrine. Paul regarded speaking in tongues as one of the gifts of the Spirit but he did not expect all to possess it. "Do all speak with tongues?" (1 Cor. 12: 30). In 1 Cor. 12: 4–11 we find a complete list of gifts and tongues is placed eighth in order. In Eph. 4: 8–13 is the condensed list of the gifts, and tongues is omitted.

My plea is for balance and tolerance in these vital matters of spiritual equipment. All are necessary. God has divided His gifts one to one, and another to another. It is obvious then that we need each other if we are all to be blessed by all He has given to His Church.

Finally, God sanctifies us that others may be sanctified. "And for their sakes I sanctify myself, that they also might be sanctified through the truth" (John 17: 19). The whole purpose of my ascent of the Inner Everest is not that I should personally, or selfishly, live closer and nearer to my Lord. I climb higher that I may help another to the same altitude. Jesus was sanctifying Himself to suffering, that the disciples also should enter into the experience of suffering, that they might also know the spiritual truth that life always comes out of death.

We can make suffering redemptive because of His sanctification. If we confirm that sanctification, it is that others also may be sanctified.

This is a new dimension of life for me. My presence at well-known conventions is not for a personal spiritual shot in the arm. I make it a place of dedication to new truth, to a new relationship with the Lord that I may go away and bring another into that truth and relationship. No more do I live for myself. My ascent ceases to be for a personal selfish spiritual acclaim, but that I may help another to stand in Christ's strength and purpose of His will, who would not have done so but for my obedience and sanctification.

I camped one year with the Worldwide Evangelization Crusade in the Isle of Anglesey. The full day out was, for me, to climb with senior campers up the Pyg track to the summit of Snowdon. I enjoyed every foot of the climb, happy hours with great fellowship. Ignoring the little cafe near the summit we climbed on and up to the trig-point and cairn another hundred feet higher.

It is also possible to reach the cafe on a narrow-gauge rack and pinion railway along the Llanberis ridge. It was a beautifully clear day and we could see for miles. But while we feasted on the view the little train puffed round the bend and wheezed to a halt at the cafe below. Some of the boys became sarcastic about "climbers" who came up in a train, rushed to fill up with fizz-pop and ice cream, and then wrote a picture postcard home with the official postmark "Summit of Snowdon" impressed over the stamp. They never moved an inch up the final 100 ft. slopes!

Suddenly we saw that a man had alighted from the train and was desperately trying to push an invalid chair up the rocky slopes. In the chair was an 18-year-old girl, no doubt paralysed in her legs. The man was getting nowhere fast. Every two feet he pushed the chair up he slipped back a foot. Without a word from me, four lads from our party jumped up and ran skidding and sliding to the despairing chair-pusher. The lads each took a wheel and lifting the chair shoulder high steadily climbed back up the slope and placed the chair right on top of the cairn! The girl was suddenly enthralled with the terrific vista. For minutes she just lived off the view. Then all confused, she realised she had not thanked her "carriers" and immediately did her best to express what was obviously a very deep gratitude. She never dreamed she would ever get to the top. Now, by their kindness, she was actually on top of the cairn on the summit! The lads felt rather awkward at all the thanks poured on them. "Forget it," said one, all red and confused. "Nothing, just nothing, Miss," exclaimed another, wishing the embarrassing appreciation would stop.

The engine hooted. The lads lifted their precious burden and, carefully treading down the stony slopes, placed the chair on the train. The engine "blew" and moved off. The lads remained waving till the train turned the bend below.

All the way back to camp the lads were talking about the day's climb. Hardly a word about their own fun and experiences, but their conversation went on like this — "She never expected to get to the top, did she!"—"Did you see her when she got on top — never a word for minutes — what a view!" — "I felt awful when she tried to thank us!" — "I guess it made her day!" Never a word about themselves. The joy of getting the girl to the top, who would never have got there but for them, was the only worthwhile event of the day.

This is it! Jesus said, "I sanctify myself that they also may be sanctified."

Am I willing for that right now? That the sanctification He effects in my life, the gifts He gives, I shall desire to use for one objective only — that others may be sanctified also.

15

Camp Seven — Vision

SURELY there is no greater thrill to a climber than to know he treads the final slopes to the summit. Long weary marches are now a memory. Necessary exacting preparations and the crossing of preliminary obstacles all lead to this great moment. This is the real climbing!

Camps seven and eight on Everest brought the assault teams within striking distance of the summit. These next two camps and summit are the most vital, challenging and rewarding of the whole expedition.

Spiritually it is the same. All that lies behind is in preparation for the last vital stage — a relationship where God works out His purpose through me. He brings me into His outworking for mankind. Redeemed and sanctified for His redemptive purpose; what a privilege! That the Almighty God should need redeemed human nature to use instrumentally for His purposes is beyond my capacity to understand. From now on I am involved in God's ways, knowing His mind, working together with Him. That humbles me if nothing else does.

First and foremost God gives vision. Although I may be ignorant of much detail I am made to see the objective and my obedience towards it. Detail comes by a daily walk in faith. Strategy I see from the very granting of the vision. Tactics are shown in my daily communion with God.

Vision is essential in this last all-important stage. The book of Proverbs, enclosing scholarly maxims, deals with my moral relationship with God and with men. One such basic premise is found in 29: 18, "Where there is no vision, the people perish." This may be ambiguous, but both ideas are true. With no vision it is failure subjectively. Without vision it is disaster objectively. It has been said tritely in modern terminology, "Aim at nothing and you will hit it every time."

General Montgomery shared his plan of advance across the Western Desert with as many of his ordinary fellow-soldiers as he could reach in the time available. He drew diagrams for them in the sand. He took them into his confidence and they responded to him and fought as never before.

Sir John Hunt, knowing his men well, could not withhold the plan too long from them. Gathering them in the tent he looked around at that group — the cream of climbers. Some sat on boxes. Others lay in sleeping bags. Tenzing stood nearby at the tent entrance. In the minds of each of them was the yet unanswered question, "What is my job to be?" It is easy for us to realise this was their paramount moment. The atmosphere was electric, though outside it hung still and sultry.

At the end of the briefing Sir John commented on the changing air of expectancy to one of calm confidence and satisfaction. Doubts had been removed. Everyone knew the official course of events for the immediate days ahead. Above all, everyone felt he had an important contribution to make towards the objectives.

In the years of my missionary experience I have often come from a planning conference with God. On occasions I knew God's directive three years ahead when often fellow missionaries under my

.leadership saw but half that time along our united task on the Tibetan Border.

Vision is seeing an objective and understanding all that is involved. The Everest climbers, rising from their boxes or crawling from their sleeping bags, gazed on the last summit stretches with a new dimension of their own personal commitment. Can I make that overhang? What if a blizzard catches us on that shoulder and the weather deteriorates — could we get back to the tents or find our way in blinding snow? If the oxygen is not enough for that final assault because the climbing takes too long, will we get back at all? The glory of the summit is balanced against the odds. There is depth in vision — not only in height.

Moses was not allowed to enter the land God promised the Israelites. But from Pisgah, the place of vision, he saw that land. "And Moses went up from the plains of Moab to Mount Nebo, to the top of Pisgah, which is opposite Jericho. And the Lord showed him all the land, Gilead as far as Dan, all Naphtali, the land of Ephraim and Manasseh, all the land of Judah as far as the Western Sea, the Negeb, and the Plain, that is, the valley of Jericho the city of palm trees, as far as Zoar. And the Lord said to him, This is the land of which I swore to Abraham, to Isaac, and to Jacob, 'I will give it to your descendants.' I have let you see it with your eyes, but you shall not go over there" (Deut. 34: 1–5).

Here is the true analysis of any vision God may give His sanctified servants. Moses was looking west; his gaze directed north-west to south-west. Follow the analysis of this wide panorama.

Gilead The mountains of Gilead, 2,000–3,000 ft. high, appear still more elevated from the west owing to the depression of the Jordan valley, and so resemble a massive wall on the horizon. But when ascended they present a wide table land tossed about in mild confusion of undulating downs with rich grass and magnificent forests.

I have trekked for years amongst the wooded slopes of the Himalayan foothills. Often with a map I would determine where a village would be but could see no sign of habitation. Sometimes rising smoke or terraced fields dug from the precipitous mountainside would be the only clue to life among the hills. So often village life is hidden from the traveller. In vision we must be assured that God is at work when no evidence points to the fact. We judge too often by what we can only see. God does His greatest work hidden from our eyes. "It is the glory of God to conceal a thing" (Proverbs 25: 2). In the lands of Bhutan and Mozambique missionary strategists evaluated nothing was possible due to governmental restrictions. When entry was eventually effected it was to find God had already begun His work in His own way through His own chosen personalities. We had deduced that there was nothing. With God there is always something. In vision always, without fail, believe where you do not see.

Naphtali was the northern border territory with heathen neighbours. The Israelites were overrun and the population decimated by the invasion of the Gentiles. Tiglath Pileser swept away its people to Assyria. It was the area of fenced cities and border skirmishes, the place of casualties. There will always be casualties in vision. I know of no road to the objective that is without bloodstains. There is a price to be paid.

What vision could be more challenging than to see

102

the Church built in war-torn Viet Nam! Over the years God has raised up that Church to His glory. I have stood beside a grave outside Da Nang of a young man who died in an ambush on a nearby pass. Standing with me was the young widow with the baby the father never saw.

On another occasion my wife and I waited till an ambulance stopped outside the Customs door of No. 3 Building of London Airport. The plane from Viet Nam had arrived with a W.E.C. family. The nurse allowed us to mount the step and look in the ambulance to see a couple with their little girl. All had been hurt, the parents particularly so, when their mission house had been blown up by the Viet Cong. There is blood in vision.

Ephraim The "precious things of the earth", "flowers", "olive valleys", and "vines", were assigned to Ephraim (Isa. 28: 1–4). Travellers attest the increasing beauty of the country as they enter Ephraim. Hills are clothed with vegetation and intersected by streams of running water. Ephraim is "doubly fruitful". Ephraim speaks of the high hills of blessing.

Thank God His vision for us is not all of hidden work and casualties. We enjoy the firstfruits as the vision becomes flesh. I well remember talking to one of our missionaries from Colombia. He recounted how they had been shamefully beaten and ill-treated at a police post late at night. Finally released, he and his Colombian co-workers staggered home to wash the blood from their bodies. Then they prayed — prayed according to their vision for Colombia, that God would give them churches of redeemed lives; printing presses to print the eternal Word; Bible Schools to train the young Colombian

103

pastors; a hospital to be a medium to reveal the love of Christ to Colombia. Today you may walk through Bogota — a high hill of fruitfulness — to see every request has been granted. Vision includes the joy of increasing fulfilment.

Manasseh was the low country bounded by sea and Mount Carmel. The name means "Trying to forget". So it is in experience in Christian work that there are low areas of tragedy which we would try to forget. We spoke of casualties in vision, and it would be wrong to omit the fact that "tragedy" is another factor we shall experience. I know few histories of fulfilled vision that have not known a tragedy. A broken heart, and sometimes a broken life wracks a soul with sobs and a fellowship with grief. Do not be lulled with the idea that the enemy of souls will allow God's work to develop uninterrupted. The devil will attack often and long to wear down the Lord's servants. Too often he gains limited victory — but to us it is a painful loss. Illustrations are difficult to give as they are redemptively locked in the minds and lives of those who seek to salvage these precious broken lives. For all concerned it is best our lips are sealed — except when we fall on our knees to pray. Moral failure, spiritual pride, selfish means and ends have all contributed their heartbreak in the pressing forward to God's objective.

Judah means "praise". Occupying a high hilly region, the tribe drove out their adversaries, retained their vigour in pastoral life and trade. They accumulated abundant wealth. Truly Judah speaks of hills of praise and blessing.

Fruitfulness and Praise are the high hills of thrilling experience. I climbed Judah recently. News has come through that our oldest field in W.E.C. in the

Congo has made a momentous decision. The field has long left the pioneering days of its founder, C. T. Studd. It has known co-operation and partnership with the several hundred ever-growing churches. Now, in spiritual maturity, the Church accepts the integration of the Mission. The Mission dies — the Church lives. The missionaries continue in their number and variety of ministries but only together with and under Congolese fellowship and direction. Praise God!

The Negeb — or the land to the South. The desert area, arid and unproductive. A true analogy of periods and areas in the work of the Lord. So in juxtaposition with fruitfulness there often remains a dry sterile area. It has been blessed with devoted missionaries of prayer and sacrificial living. It has enjoyed all that fruitful lands have received — but with no result. A sterile Muslim area may not be far distant from thousands of animists rejoicing in a new-found Christ as the Spirit of God is outpoured. It is not for us to question God's sovereignty; of this we are warned in Isa. 45: 11, "Would you dare question me concerning my children, or instruct me in my handiwork?" But there is held out to us the promise that the desert will blossom like a rose. God has His timing — but for us there may be a time of dryness and drought until. . . .

The Plains or The Crescent was the valley of Jericho bordering the Dead Sea. Moses, looking immediately down from his high vantage point, over-looked the Jordon valley. At the southern end were the sites of the old cities of Sodom and Gomorrah.

The record of these cities reminds us of such sin and debauchery that God had to destroy them. The book of the Revelation speaks of places "where

Satan's seat is". Satan is not omnipresent. His seat of power and control often appears centralised in different world areas.

So it is in vision. Some time, somewhere, we feel the very hard core of Satanic opposition, the focal points from which stem every plan and attempt to overthrow God's will and purpose. At times it is fierce and the battle spiritually is hand to hand with evil powers in heavenly places. There is no question of defeat. God has ever promised, concerning His work, that "the gates of hell shall not prevail against it." (Matt. 16: 18). The word "gate" means the wisdom and plans of the enemy. In the Lord's day the wise men judged the legal cases of the town at the "gate" and in this way the term enriched its meaning.

Vision is real to the one to whom God entrusts His purpose. Neither is there any misunderstanding concerning the cost it may exact, but there is also no existence of doubt that the spiritual objective will finally fly the banner of the Cross.

16

Camp Eight — Identification

THE CLIMBERS of Everest were fourteen in all. Only seven climbers, with their indomitable Sherpa companions-cum-carriers, put foot on the final pyramid leading to the summit. Of the seven climbers four only reached the South Summit (28,700 ft.): Bourdillon, Evans, Hillary and Tenzing. It is well known to all that Hillary and Tenzing were the successful "summitters". It must be quickly explained that the plan of an assault on a peak seldom allows every climber to reach the objective. The majority are in support. The successful are only there because of a team's co-operative effort, and none realise it more than those who, gasping, bend over their ice-axes, and with hammering hearts, know the mountain is all below them. Yet, even so, plans have to be adjusted as personnel are eliminated, because of lack of acclimatisation, injury and personality problems, as the climb develops.

Spiritually only the latter half of the simile is true. It is God's intent that all should conquer their Inner Everest. This is clearly seen as God reveals His purpose through the chosen nation — the Jews. Will you follow me through a few references?

God's purpose for mankind worldwide "Now the Lord said to Abram, Go from your country and your kindred and your father's house to the land that I will show you. And I will make of you a great nation, and I will bless you, and make your name great, so that you will be a blessing. I will bless those who bless you, and him who curses you I will curse; and by you all the families of the earth shall bless themselves" (Gen. 12: 1–3).

God intended every man to be a priest and citizen of a holy nation "If only you will now listen to me and keep my covenant, then out of all peoples you shall become my special possession; for the whole earth is mine. You shall be my kingdom of priests, my holy nation" (Exod. 19: 5, 6).

The Israelites — the Jewish nation — refused this privilege and purpose "And they (the Israelites) stood afar off, and said to Moses, You speak to us, and we will hear; but let not God speak to us, lest we die" (Exod. 20: 19). "The Lord spoke with you face to face at the mountain, out of the midst of the fire, while I stood between the Lord and you at that time, to declare to you the word of the Lord; for you were afraid because of the fire, and you did not go up into the mountain" (Deut. 5: 4, 5). "Now therefore why should we die? For this great fire will consume us; if we hear the voice of the Lord our God any more, we shall die. For who is there of all flesh, that has heard the voice of the living God speaking out of the midst of fire, as we have, and has still lived? Go near, and hear all that the Lord our God will say; and speak to us all that the Lord our God will speak to you; and we will hear and do it" (Deut. 5: 25–27).

Thus it is today. God's purpose and plan: the sacrifice of His Son; the sending of His Holy Spirit; the granting of spiritual gifts. His grace, love, power and glory are not for the limited objective of forgiveness of sins and renewed fellowship with God, but that we may *all* tread the summit of our own Everest, and be fully relevant and involved in God's purpose through us. We eliminate ourselves in any failure to climb high.

God forbid that I should judge, for I humbly and honestly evaluate my own spiritual altitude, but so few tread the final slopes. Only a handful are summitters — and the next chapter reveals the qualification. The true Church of Jesus Christ seldom seems to climb above Camp Four. Maybe the clouds and mists of ignorance hide the higher altitudes from their upward look; an ignorance created by a lack of personal reading and study of the Word of God, ignorance confirmed by the preaching of an emasculated Gospel.

Failure to climb high is due to personal unwillingness to accept the full conditions of discipleship. The Church of Jesus Christ today declares by its very life that He is not "Lord" — however much it so assents in prayer and worship.

Vision is a terrific, inspiring and challenging view from a high vantage point. Identification is the costly price to pay to be oriented in the vision. God now places us positionally in His work. The Commander-in-Chief indicates my fighting post.

I want you to see three men in Scripture taking up these positions of identification at the vital point of their ministry. "The Spirit lifted me up and took me away, and I went in bitterness in the heat of my spirit, the hand of the Lord being strong upon me; and I came to the exiles at Telabib, who dwelt by the river Chebar. And I sat there overwhelmed among them seven days" (Ezek. 3: 14–16).

Ezekiel, a prophet and reformer, is made relevant to the exiles from Palestine. He had to speak to them with the objective of bringing obedience and repentance that were the only conditions for restoration and pardon. He had to speak intelligently and logically from a firm base of personal experience. Thus he "sat with them" silent, learning, experiencing the lot and thought of the exiles. *Then* the word of the Lord was given him.

Hosea had to identify himself with faithless Israel so that God could show them His filial love through His prophet's enacting their condition. "The Lord said to me, Go again and love a woman loved by another man, an adulteress, and love her as I, the Lord, love the Israelites although they resort to other gods and love the raisin-cakes offered to their idols. So I got her back for fifteen pieces of silver, a homer of barley and a measure of wine; and I said to her, Many a long day you shall live in my house and not play the wanton, and have no intercourse with a man, nor I with you. For the Israelites shall live many a long day without king or prince, without sacrifice or sacred pillar, without image or household gods; but after that they will again seek the Lord their God and David their king, and turn anxiously to the Lord for his bounty in days to come" (Hos. 3: 1–5).

What a costly, distasteful relationship the holy man of God had to accept that the lesson of God's deep faithful love could be spelt out in terms clearly to be understood. There was no other way to get the truth home.

The Lord Jesus Christ Himself reveals true identification in this wonderful record. "Let Christ Jesus be your example as to what your attitude should be. For he, who had always been God by nature, did not cling to his prerogatives as God's equal, but stripped himself of all privilege by consenting to be a slave by nature and being born as mortal man. And, having become man, he humbled himself by living a life of utter obedience, even to the

110

extent of dying, and the death he died was the death of a common criminal. That is why God has now lifted him so high, and has given him the name beyond all names, so that at the name of Jesus 'every knee shall bow', whether in heaven or earth or under the earth. And that is why, in the end, 'every tongue shall confess' that Jesus Christ is the Lord, to the glory of God the Father" (Phil. 2: 5–11).

You and I can understand this more clearly than the previous examples because we are the ones receiving His identification. The one ground of hope, comfort and faith lies in this supreme truth that identifying Himself with me He leads me out of the crevasse of sin and condemnation to the heights of life in its utter and complete fulfilment.

Now comes the crunch. "For I have given you an example, that you also should do as I have done to you" (John 13: 15). I have to go down as well. This touches almost every aspect of my life, including wife and family, dress, security and those aspects of life we glibly call our "rights".

In contemplating the outworking of this identification I know of no better illustration than as follows. In a leprosarium in Chandag, Almora district of India, lived Mary Reed. It is her life I would like to spell out more fully and share with you my meeting her.

I had commenced a long march well before dawn. Looking at the great snow ranges it seemed as if a giant were striding along the great Himalaya Range, splashing the high peaks with a pink wash. The sun was rising for another wonderful October day. Villages were now stirring. Pack animals passed me on the narrow ledge road that was taking us due north, deeper and deeper into the higher ranges.

About mid-afternoon we came through a low pass

into the beautiful Pithoragarh Valley. My eyes were automatically drawn towards the western hills and followed the road winding like a scar up its steepness. At the top, where the road disappears from view, was a lonely, lovely copse of deodar trees and the glint of a white-washed house coloured by the low sun. "Not far now, Sahib," said my coolie. "We should be in by sundown and the climb will be in the shade."

After a rest, I flung my rucksack on to my back and determined that the next stop of this tiring day would be the end of the trail. I began to conjecture in my mind about the lady I was to meet and under whose hospitality I was to stay that night. Mary Reed was an aged missionary from America. Some years back she had returned to India after furlough with a new venture and a new reason for the venture!

Mary had been a wonderful missionary. Her love for the Lord was infectious. Her patience was almost provoking, for it was an example which made all who met her feel uncomfortable. There was neither sick nor sorrowing that Mary Reed did not touch with love and help, until she was loved by all.

Washing her hands one day, she noticed on her wrist a little discoloration that did not yield to soap and water. Day by day she watched it with deepening concern. She noticed that this particular patch became insensitive to feeling. It was convincing in its symptoms. There could be one diagnosis — leprosy!

Furlough was nearly due, so with much care in the cleanliness of her clothes and tableware, she quietly carried on until the day when she could consult a leading skin specialist in the United States.

The doctor buttoned her cuff and, gravely looking at Mary, said, "I do not know how to share my deep conviction about this trouble, Mary." She smiled and replied, "I know, Doctor, but I think you can safely tell me. It is leprosy, is it not?" A significant pause was broken by his slow reply, "Well, we must await final tests, but the signs are very serious and ominous."

The tests supported the symptoms. Mary had contracted leprosy. What to do now? Kind friends offered every facility for the condition to be treated at the best place, by the best doctors. But Mary took the whole matter much more seriously. Why had God allowed this to happen? What was His purpose in it all? Quietly listening, she heard the Divine direction to return to India and a new venture in caring for leprosy patients.

Mary observed medical advice and took the medicines prescribed. The best she could hope for was an arresting of the disease, the worst development of the disease which could mar and scar a lovely life. Mary went back to Chandag, which was the white-washed building just above us in the setting sun.

Coolies and pony-men followed me through the gates into the little cluster of houses. Each room harboured a man or woman who had little hope of ever returning symptom-free to his or her own village.

Mary was waiting for me in the doorway, with a wonderful smile of greeting. I knew she would not shake hands with me. In His grace and goodness God had not allowed the disease to progress. There still remained just a patch on the wrist. But Mary took no chances with others.

It was lovely to be with her. She knew how tired I was. I had a delicious hot bath in a zinc tub and then the soft oil lamps bathed the table in a quiet light. This was heaven. Mary could only speak of the

113

Lord's goodness to her, and the fragrance of Christ hung over the little colony on the ridge. It was a fragrance as marked as the lavender-scented sheets I slipped my tired body into that night, soon to fall asleep.

The next day was Sunday. The sun streamed through the window. The Himalayas glistened as the sun kissed the snowy peaks. The chapel bell sent a happy note at intervals across the valley. Mary and I stood in the chapel porch and watched the little population of the colony come slowly towards the House of God. It seemed all of them had been marked by leprosy. Some crawled along on stumps; others hobbled. But the limitations which we might call tragedies were lost behind radiant smiles and happy greetings of "Salaam, Sahib! Salaam, Memsahib!" Not a sorrowing face could be seen; only triumph and gratitude were visible.

I could not sing. I had to watch them when their eyes were shut in prayer. There was a lump in my throat as stumped wrists and deformed fingers pushed over the pages of their own Bibles. I know the singing was thin, but that morning's worship was accepted in heaven.

Marred hands dropped tithes into the bag as it was passed around. But their hearts were unscarred and full of love. The love of Mary Reed's Saviour had reached a hundred others.

I was further north when news of her death came. A day came when we quietly stood at the grave on the ridge in the colony not far from the white-washed house that was again colouring in the sunset.

I saw Jesus in that life and I shall never forget her — Mary Reed of Chandag, who in the fullest way she knew possible followed that Example.

17

The Summit — Intercession

EDMUND HILLARY relates in *High Adventure* the last slog to the ice dome of Everest, "To my right a slender snow ridge climbed up to a snowy dome about forty feet above our heads. But all the way along the ridge the thought had haunted me that the summit might be the crest of a cornice. It was too late to take risks now. I asked Tenzing to belay me strongly, and I started cutting a cautious line of steps up the ridge. Peering from side to side and thrusting with my ice-axe, I tried to discover a possible cornice, but everything seemed solid and firm. I waved Tenzing up to me. A few more whacks of the ice-axe, a few very weary steps, and we were on the summit of Everest."

There is little parallel here with our own spiritual progress, but I mention this incident only to emphasise that the authority to say Everest was climbed could only come from the two weary men themselves. Here then is my difficulty. How may I speak of a summit I have not yet myself put underfoot? There is a long slog beyond the camp Identification to the summit. I may know progress towards God moving and working in me and through me in His perfect and delightful purpose for my life. But there are degrees even in this. There are many halting places between the last camp and the summit, where I may say, often physically and mentally weary, "I can go no further." But this is an Absolute, and Ultimate — a point where God is fully expressing His redemptive love and power through this sanctified bit of humanity I call "me." I can only say what others have said of this objective. I can only point to it. First then, are there any who have gained this spiritual summit? The full answer is only known by God Himself. But I know that they need not be well-known men and women of God. A poor widow or mother could know the summit as she has interceded for a son or daughter. Such a life is hidden from our knowledge in the mass of an exploding population.

This Absolute is the present life of our Lord before the throne of God our Father finding expression also through us. He shares with us His priesthood according to the writer of the Hebrews. This injects a serious relevancy into any one of my circumstances. A priest is an Intercessor. An Intercessor is one who recognises that he is set apart by God to bridge the gap between needy souls and God. With one hand an Intercessor grips his burden and with the other reaches out to grip the Almighty God through the authority of the Lord Jesus Christ, Saviour of the World, Intercessor of Mankind.

An Intercessor feels specifically relevant to his situation and not the result of an accident of circumstances. Norman Grubb in his book *God Unlimited* puts it in better words than I could possibly express: "An Intercessor is not a vague drifter, just passively yielding to some difficult situation. He is a person with a purpose because the purposing Christ is within him." Yes, it is life with a purpose. We know what God is after and we are willing to pay any price God may ask to reach it. "Who for the joy that was set before him endured the cross" (Heb. 12: 2). Life has made a complete circle. God is love. Love is self-giving, and by His sacrifice

116

He has won me back to Himself when I had become His enemy. Now He lives in me, loves through me and gives Himself again as He causes me to give to others that they also may come to Him. Thus the cycle of intercession goes on in everlasting redeeming momentum.

There are two summitters I want to introduce. Moses surely was led to the Absolute, the Ultimate, when God's almighty love wrung these words from his lips. "The next day Moses said to the people, 'You have committed a great sin. I shall now go up to the Lord; perhaps I may be able to secure pardon for your sin.' So Moses returned to the Lord and said 'O hear me! This people has committed a great sin: they have made themselves gods of gold. If thou wilt forgive them, forgive. But if not, blot out my name, I pray, from thy book which thou hast written' " (Exod. 32: 30–32). Paul's footprints marked the little-trod summit when he also pleaded, "Before Christ and my own conscience in the Holy Spirit I assure you that I am speaking the plain truth when I say that there is something that makes me feel very depressed, like a pain that never leaves me. It is the condition of my brothers and fellow-Israelites, and I have actually reached the pitch of wishing myself cut off from Christ if it meant that they could be won for God" (Rom. 9: 1–3).

Intercession touches the eternal darkness that others may have Eternal Light. Who knows anything of this?

As I trekked deep into the Himalaya I would, as direction and distance allowed, visit an aged saint of God, Mr. Grundy. He was one of the early pioneers of The Salvation Army in India. Later he resigned from The Salvation Army and began a work deep in these mountain ranges. I well remember

117

setting off early one Sunday morning to get there in time for the service. I was cutting it fine timewise and so loped along at a good four miles an hour. About three miles off I caught the glint of sun reflected on a shining surface — then the hill breeze carried to me the sound of drums and wind instruments. Soon I distinguished figures and saw a flag fully extended in the wind. I laughed as I realised Mr. Grundy had no other conception of Christian life but the Army life, and here the hill tribes reflected the Army life at any Citadel. I enjoyed that morning worship. I joined in the Hindi equivalents to "Hallelujah", "Amen", "Fire a Volley!" I finished up standing on a chair waving a handkerchief and praising the Lord. Next day I trekked on.

A few months later I learned of the death of Mr. Grundy, so on my return from the Tibetan Border I detoured to visit the family and offer my consolation. The eldest son, Mark, took me outside and told me to follow him. We climbed zig-zagging up a steep mountain cliff to a knife-edge ridge that acted as a spur and jutted out as a rocky peninsula over deep valleys. It was also a view-point for hundreds of miles of tangled Himalayan peaks, hills, valleys and villages. The world lay at our feet.

Mark pointed out a small well-worn path that ran for about 200 yards along the ridge terminating at a large sloping rock. He told me that his father used to go there almost daily at dawn to commune with God and pray at this rock. I walked to the rock feeling it to be holy ground. From the rock the view was tremendous, not only far distant, but at my feet. The rough rock was smooth in two patches where a man's knees had supported him in intercession for the world below. Praying until rough rock was worn smooth — and not just that rock, but also until the rough resistance of human hearts gave way to the touch of the Saviour.

Do I know intercession such as this? As our fellowship together comes to a close, will you kneel with me — a fellow climber? The entreaty of Andrew Murray is the entreaty of my heart, and will be also of yours. Let us pray together.

"O most blessed God! dost Thou in very deed ask me to come and give myself, my very life, wholly, even unto the death, to Thee for my fellow men? If I have heard the words of the Master aright, Thou dost indeed seek nothing less.

"O God! wilt Thou indeed have me? Wilt Thou in very deed in Christ permit me, like Him, as a member of His body, to live and die for those around me? to lay myself, I say it in deep reverence, beside Him on the altar of death, crucified with Him, and be a living sacrifice to Thee for men? Lord! I do praise Thee for this most wonderful grace. And now I come, Lord God! and give myself. Oh for the grace of Thy Holy Spirit to make the transaction definite and real! Lord, here I am, given up to Thee, to live only for those whom Thou art seeking to save."